SIMPLE
—FINGERSTYLE GUITAR SONGS—

ISBN 978-1-7051-1092-8

Visit Hal Leonard Online at
www.halleonard.com

World headquarters, contact:
Hal Leonard
7777 West Bluemound Road
Milwaukee, WI 53213
Email: info@halleonard.com

In Europe, contact:
Hal Leonard Europe Limited
42 Wigmore Street
Marylebone, London, W1U 2RY
Email: info@halleonardeurope.com

In Australia, contact:
Hal Leonard Australia Pty. Ltd.
4 Lentara Court
Cheltenham, Victoria, 3192 Australia
Email: info@halleonard.com.au

Guitar Notation Legend

THE MUSICAL STAFF shows pitches and rhythms and is divided by bar lines into measures. Pitches are named after the first seven letters of the alphabet.

TABLATURE graphically represents the guitar fingerboard. Each horizontal line represents a string, and each number represents a fret.

4th string, 2nd fret | 1st & 2nd strings open, played together | open D chord

HALF-STEP BEND: Strike the note and bend up 1/2 step.

WHOLE-STEP BEND: Strike the note and bend up one step.

GRACE NOTE BEND: Strike the note and immediately bend up as indicated.

SLIGHT (MICROTONE) BEND: Strike the note and bend up 1/4 step.

BEND AND RELEASE: Strike the note and bend up as indicated, then release back to the original note. Only the first note is struck.

PRE-BEND: Bend the note as indicated, then strike it.

VIBRATO: The string is vibrated by rapidly bending and releasing the note with the fretting hand.

PALM MUTING: The note is partially muted by the pick hand lightly touching the string(s) just before the bridge.

HAMMER-ON: Strike the first (lower) note with one finger, then sound the higher note (on the same string) with another finger by fretting it without picking.

PULL-OFF: Place both fingers on the notes to be sounded. Strike the first note and without picking, pull the finger off to sound the second (lower) note.

LEGATO SLIDE: Strike the first note and then slide the same fret-hand finger up or down to the second note. The second note is not struck.

SHIFT SLIDE: Same as legato slide, except the second note is struck.

TRILL: Very rapidly alternate between the notes indicated by continuously hammering on and pulling off.

TAPPING: Hammer ("tap") the fret indicated with the pick-hand index or middle finger and pull off to the note fretted by the fret hand.

NATURAL HARMONIC: Strike the note while the fret-hand lightly touches the string directly over the fret indicated.

PINCH HARMONIC: The note is fretted normally and a harmonic is produced by adding the edge of the thumb or the tip of the index finger of the pick hand to the normal pick attack.

TREMOLO PICKING: The note is picked as rapidly and continuously as possible.

VIBRATO BAR DIVE AND RETURN: The pitch of the note or chord is dropped a specified number of steps (in rhythm), then returned to the original pitch.

VIBRATO BAR SCOOP: Depress the bar just before striking the note, then quickly release the bar.

VIBRATO BAR DIP: Strike the note and then immediately drop a specified number of steps, then release back to the original pitch.

Additional Musical Definitions

 (accent) • Accentuate note (play it louder).

 (staccato) • Play the note short.

D.S. al Coda • Go back to the sign (𝄌), then play until the measure marked "***To Coda***," then skip to the section labelled "**Coda**."

D.C. al Fine • Go back to the beginning of the song and play until the measure marked "***Fine***" (end).

Fill • Label used to identify a brief melodic figure which is to be inserted into the arrangement.

N.C. • Harmony is implied.

 • Repeat measures between signs.

 • When a repeated section has different endings, play the first ending only the first time and the second ending only the second time.

Ain't No Sunshine

Words and Music by Bill Withers

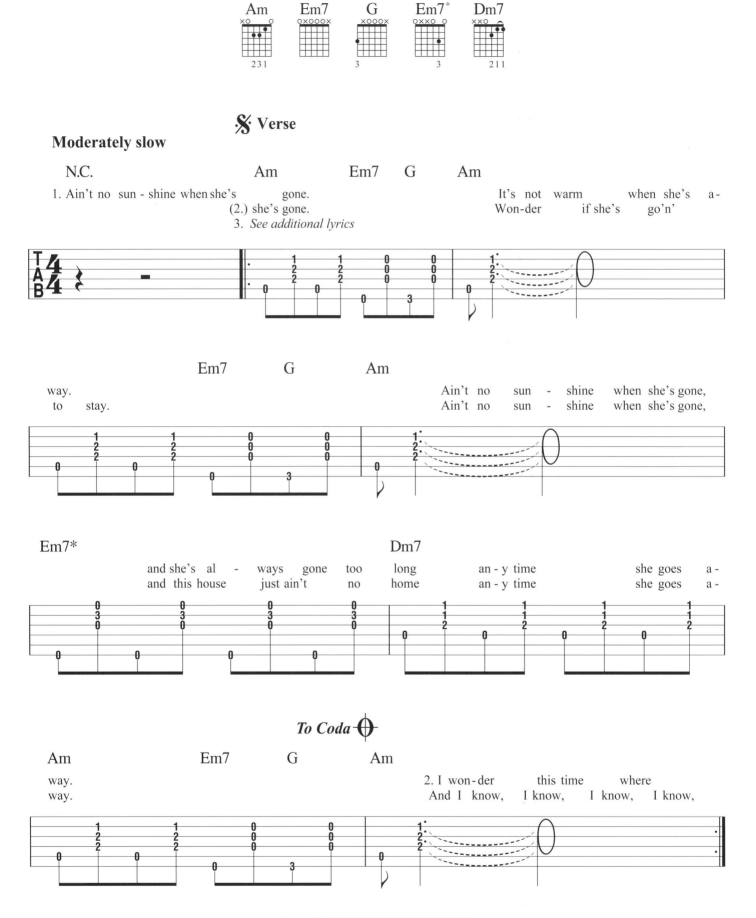

Bridge

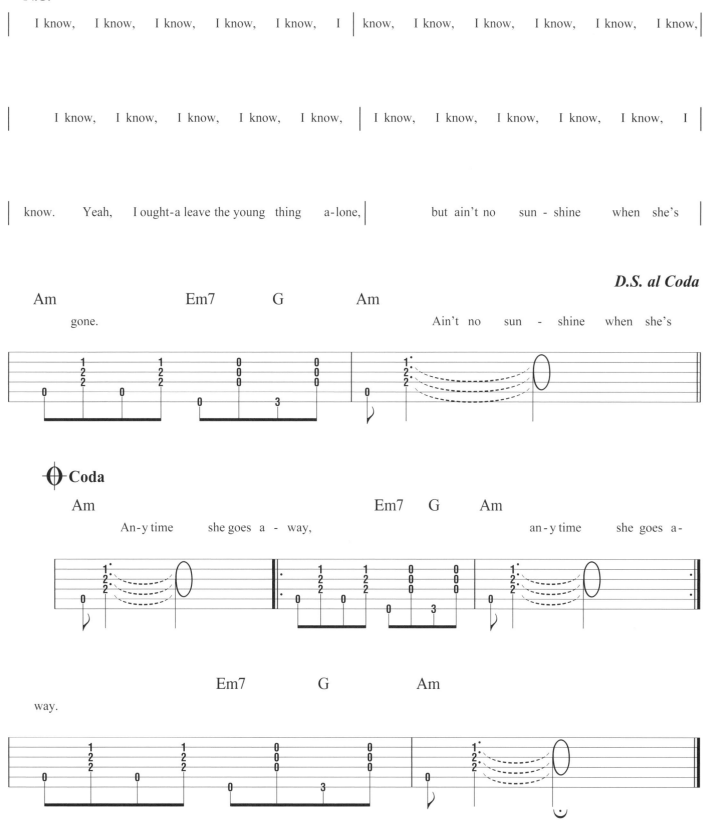

N.C.

I know, I know, I know, I know, I know, I | know, I know, I know, I know, I know, I know,

I know, I know, I know, I know, I know, | I know, I know, I know, I know, I know, I |

know. Yeah, I ought-a leave the young thing a-lone, but ain't no sun - shine when she's

D.S. al Coda

Am   Em7   G   Am

gone.   Ain't no sun - shine when she's

Coda

Am   Em7   G   Am

An-y time   she goes a - way,   an-y time   she goes a-

Em7   G   Am

way.

Additional Lyrics

3. Ain't no sunshine when she's gone,
   Only darkness every day.
   Ain't no sunshine when she's gone,
   And this house just ain't no home
   Any time she goes away. *(To Coda)*

5

Blowin' in the Wind

Words and Music by Bob Dylan

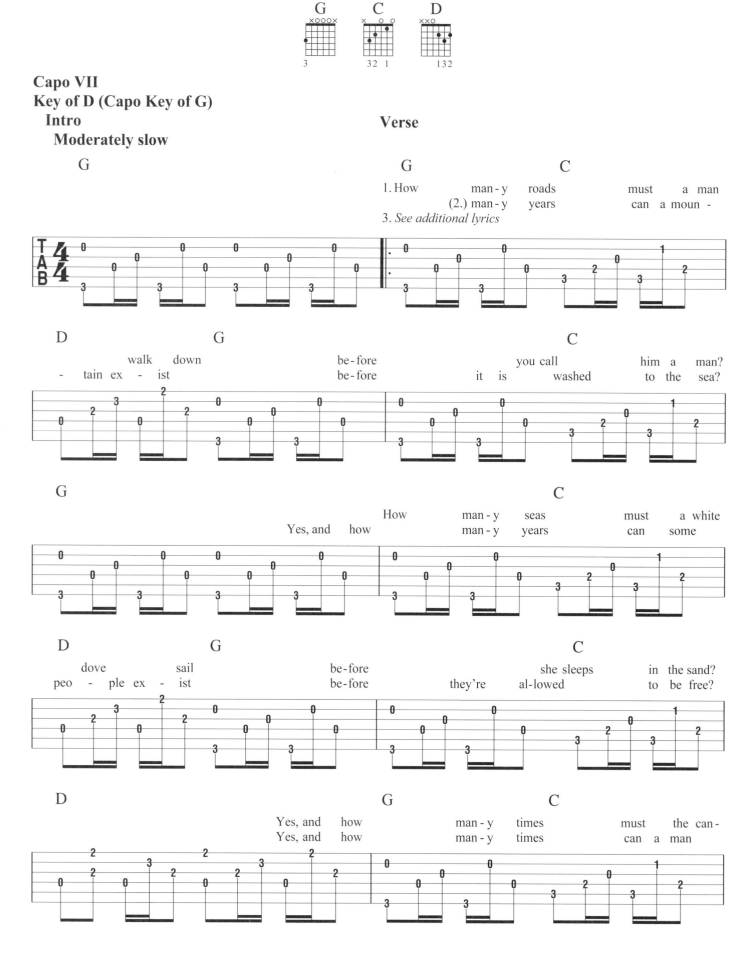

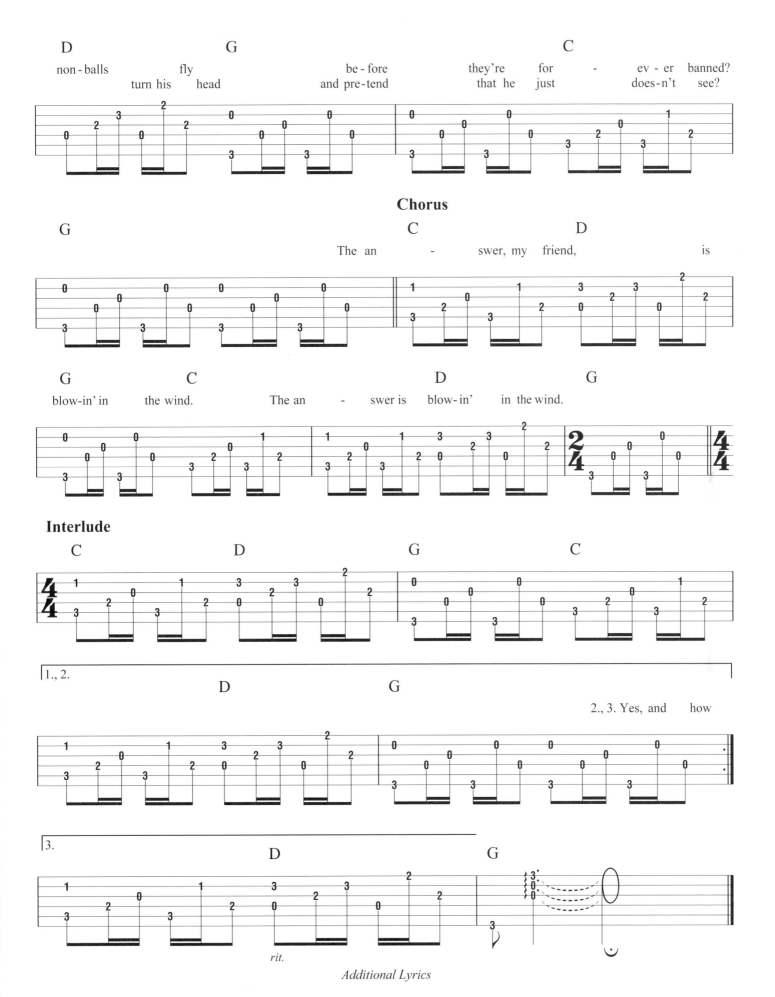

Additional Lyrics

3. Yes, and how many times must a man look up
   Before he can see the sky?
   Yes, and how many ears must one man have
   Before he can hear people cry?
   Yes, and how many deaths will it take 'til he knows
   That too many people have died?

Bridge Over Troubled Water

Words and Music by Paul Simon

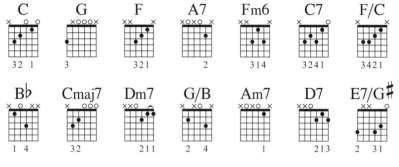

Capo III

Key of E♭ (Capo Key of C)

Intro

Moderately slow

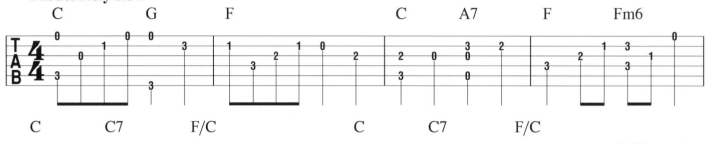

1. When you're

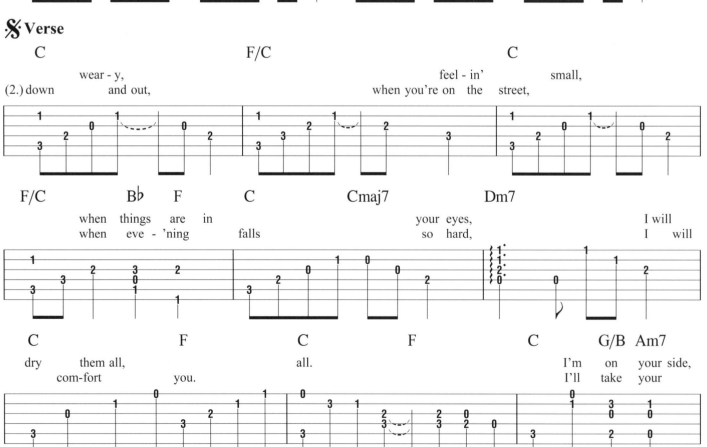

% **Verse**

C   F/C   C

     wear - y,   feel - in'   small,

(2.) down   and out,   when you're on the street,

F/C   B♭   F   C   Cmaj7   Dm7

when things are in   your eyes,   I will

when eve - 'ning falls   so hard,   I will

C   F   C   F   C   G/B   Am7

dry them all,   all.   I'm on your side,

com-fort   you.   I'll take your

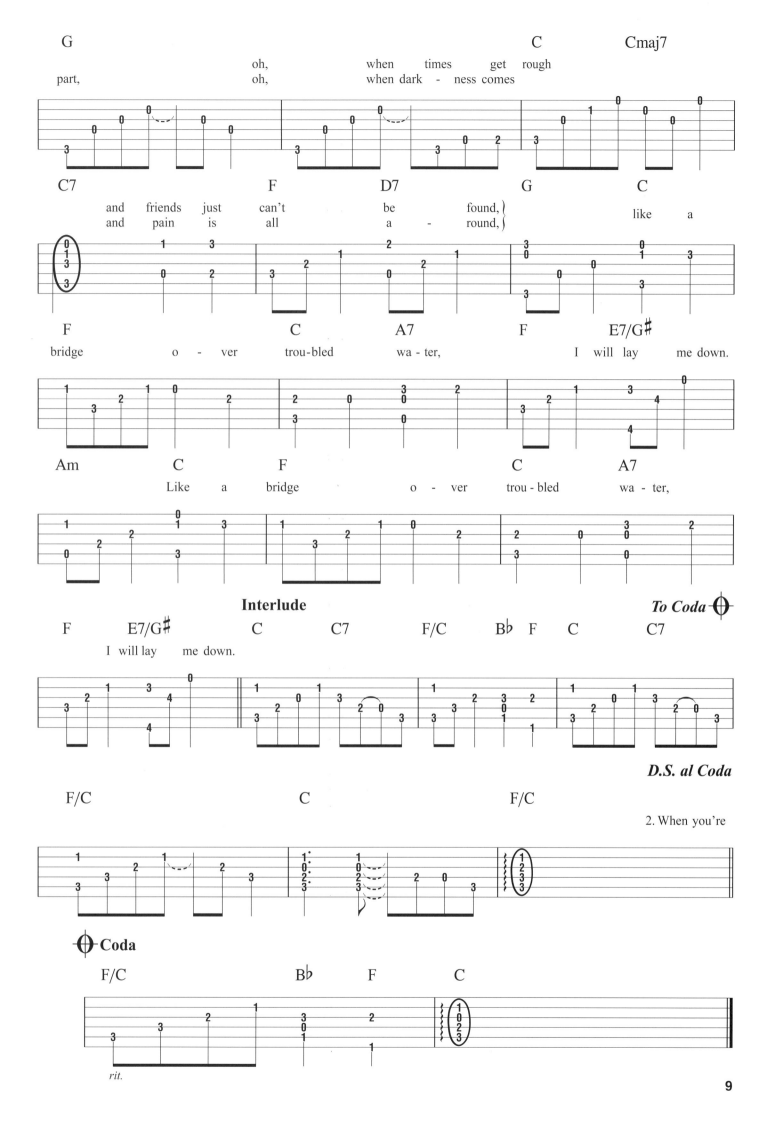

Can You Feel the Love Tonight

from THE LION KING

Music by Elton John
Lyrics by Tim Rice

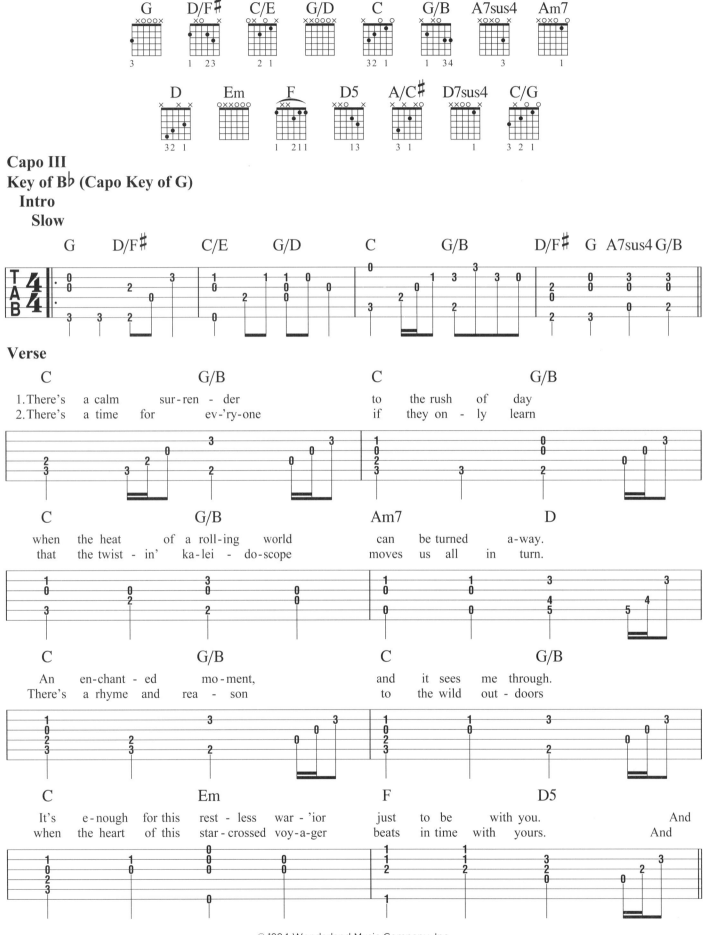

Chorus

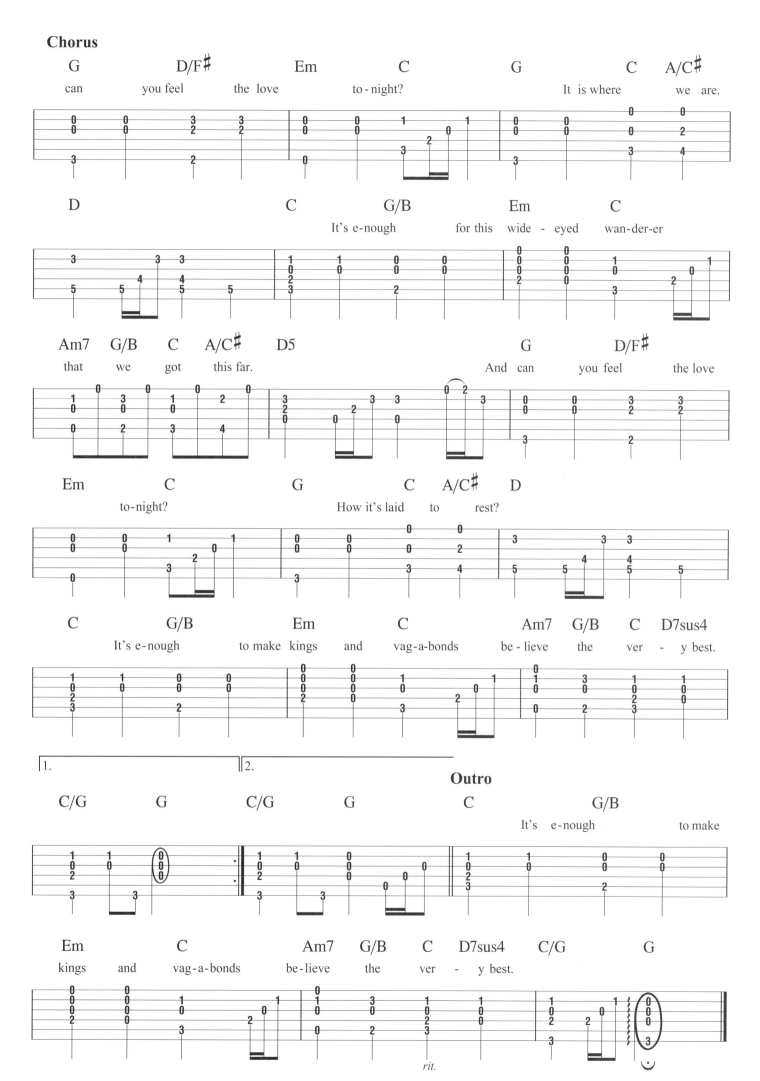

Can't Help Falling in Love

from the Paramount Picture BLUE HAWAII
Words and Music by George David Weiss, Hugo Peretti and Luigi Creatore

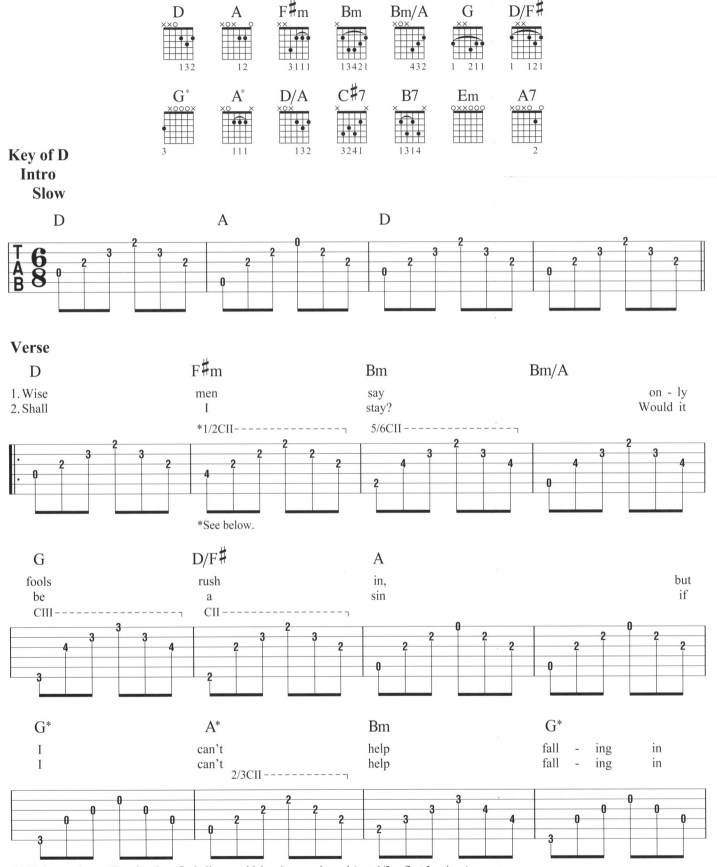

*"C" denotes barre. Fractional prefix indicates which strings are barred (e.g. 1/2 = first 3 strings).
Roman numeral suffix indicates barred fret.

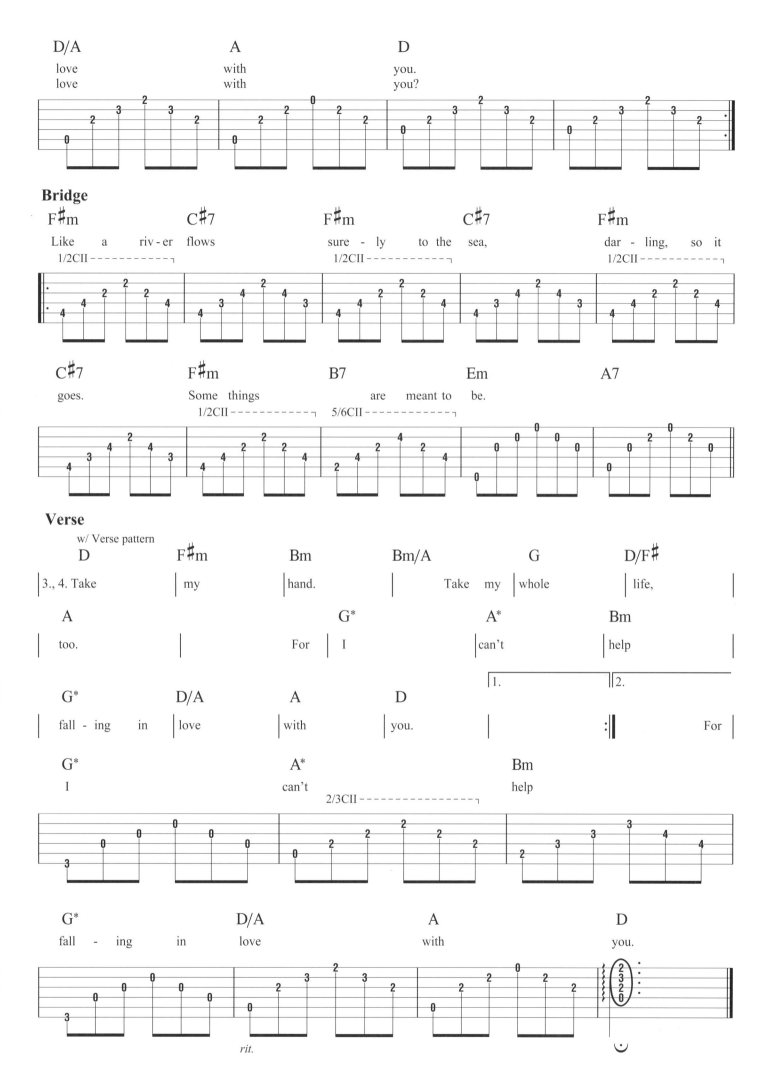

D/A　　　　　　　**A**　　　　　　　**D**
love　　　　　　with　　　　　　you.
love　　　　　　with　　　　　　you?

Bridge

F♯m　　　　　　**C♯7**　　　　**F♯m**　　　　**C♯7**　　　　**F♯m**
Like a riv-er flows　　　sure-ly to the sea,　　　dar-ling, so it
1/2CII- - - - - - - - - - - ¬　　1/2CII- - - - - - - - - ¬　　1/2CII- - - - - - - - - ¬

C♯7　　　　　**F♯m**　　　　**B7**　　　　**Em**　　　**A7**
goes.　　　Some things　　　are meant to be.
　　　　　　1/2CII- - - - - - - - ¬　5/6CII- - - - - - - - ¬

Verse

w/ Verse pattern

D　　　　**F♯m**　　**Bm**　　　**Bm/A**　　　　**G**　　　**D/F♯**
|3., 4. Take　　|my　　|hand.　　|　　Take my |whole　　|life,　　|

A　　　　　　　　**G*** 　　　**A***　　　**Bm**
|too.　　|　　For |I　　|can't　　|help　　|

　　　　　　　　　　　　　　　　　　　　1.　　　　2.

G*　　**D/A**　　　**A**　　　**D**
|fall - ing in |love　　|with　　|you.　　|　　　:|| 　　For |

G*　　　　　　**A***　　　**Bm**
I　　　　　　can't　　　help
　　　　　　2/3CII- - - - - - - - - - ¬

G*　　　　　　**D/A**　　　**A**　　　**D**
fall - ing in　　love　　　with　　　you.

rit.

13

Canon in D

By Johann Pachelbel

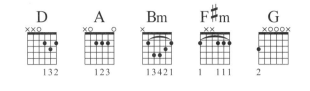

Key of D

Slow

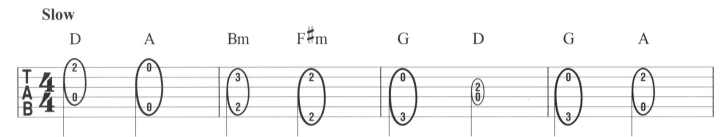

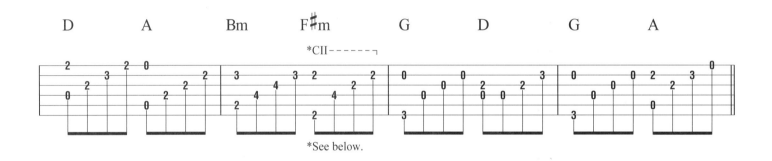

*See below.

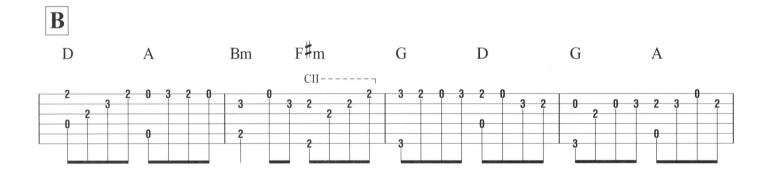

*"C" denotes barre. Fractional prefix indicates which strings are barred (e.g. 1/2 = first 3 strings).
  Roman numeral suffix indicates barred fret.

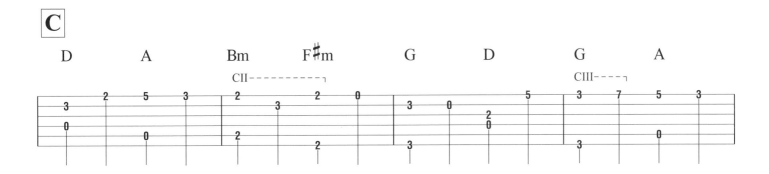

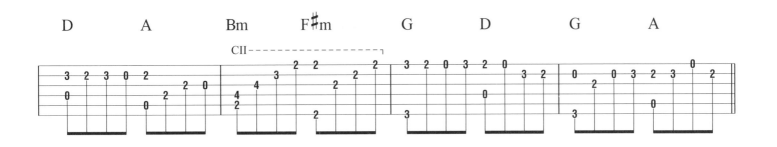

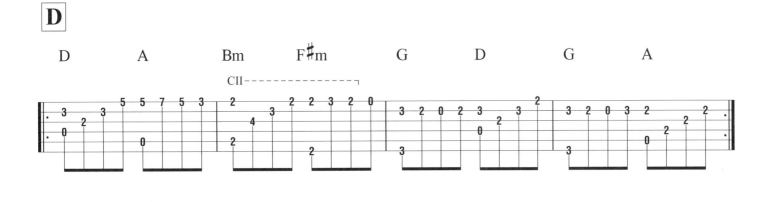

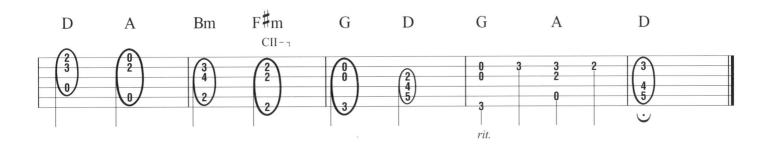

Don't Know Why

Words and Music by Jesse Harris

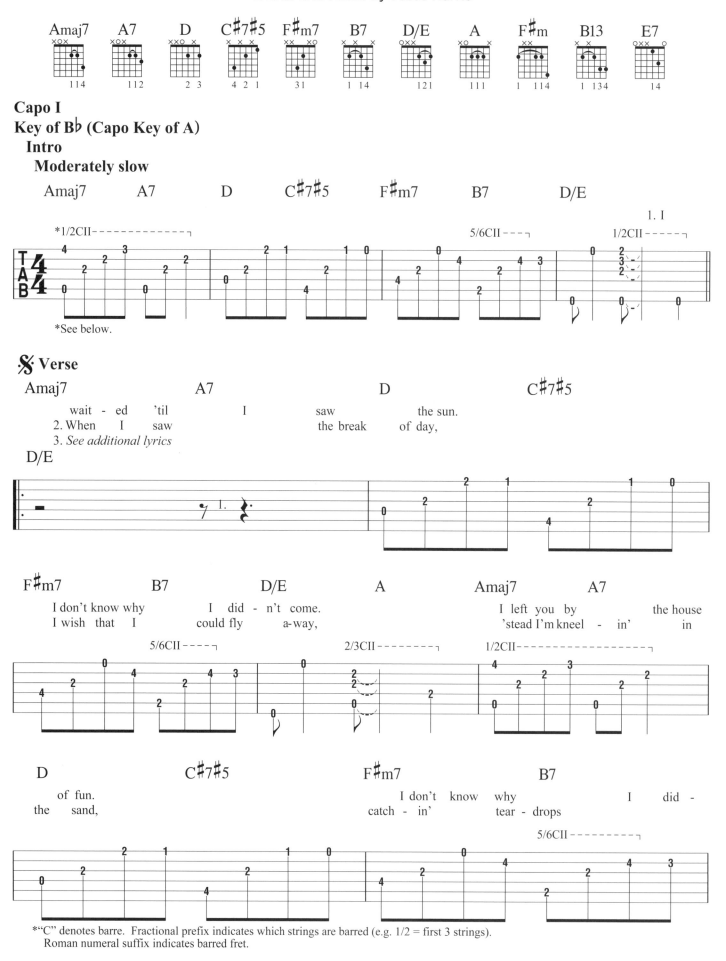

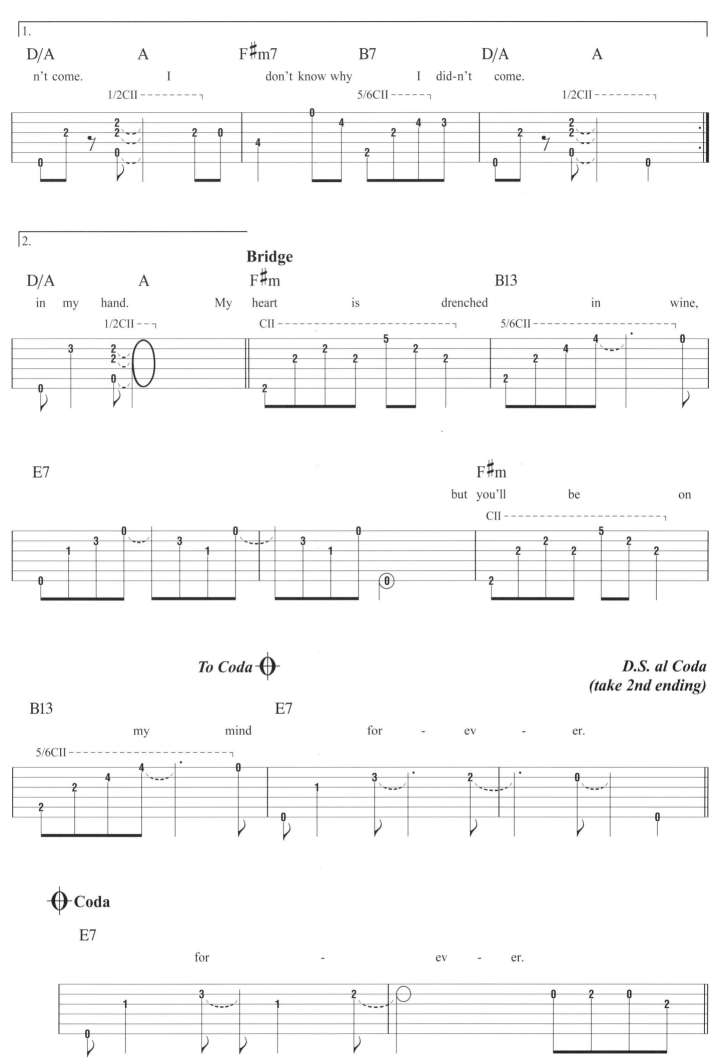

Instrumental

w/ Intro pattern

‖: Amaj7   A7 | D   C#7#5 | F#m7   B7 | D/E   :‖

Verse

w/ Verse pattern

Amaj7   A7   D   C#7#5   F#m7   B7   D/E   A

| 4. Some-thin' has   to   make | you run. | I don't know why   I did- | n't come.   I |

Amaj7   A7   D   C#7#5

   feel   as   emp   -   ty   as   a drum.

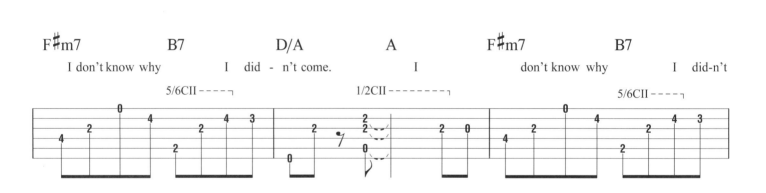

F#m7   B7   D/A   A   F#m7   B7

I don't know why   I   did - n't come.   I   don't know why   I   did-n't

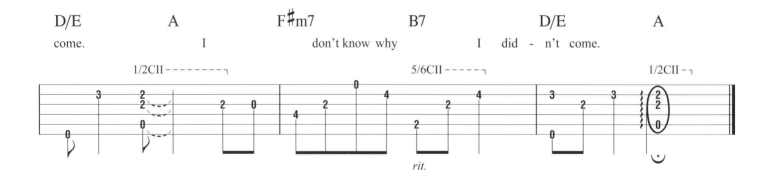

D/E   A   F#m7   B7   D/E   A

come.   I   don't know why   I   did - n't   come.

rit.

Additional Lyrics

3. Out across the endless sea,
   I would die in ecstasy.
   But I'll be a bag of bones,
   Drivin' down the road alone.

Every Breath You Take

Music and Lyrics by Sting

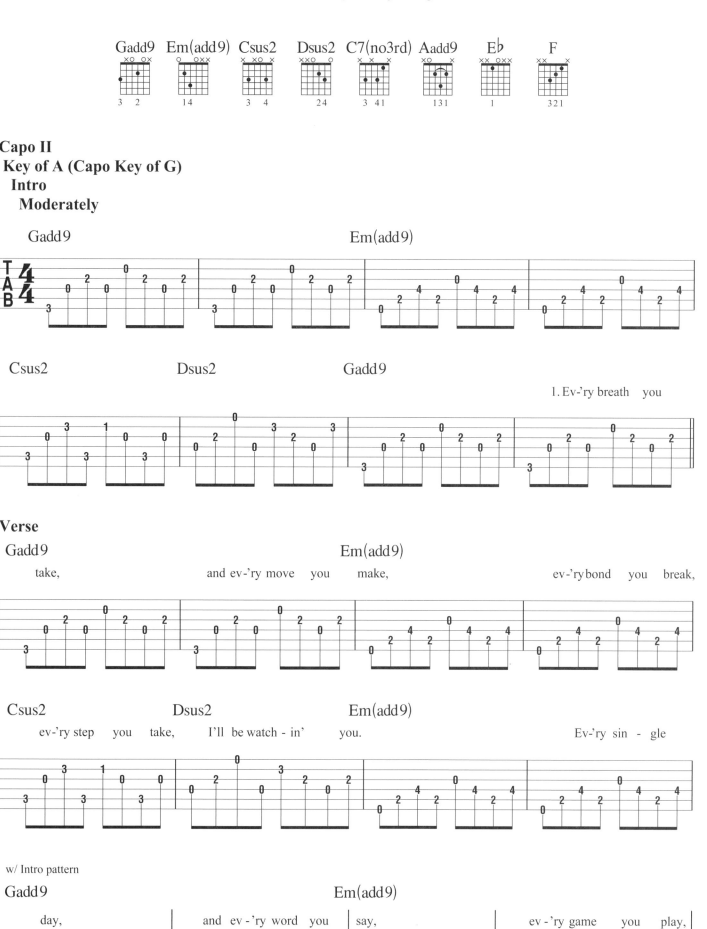

Csus2   Dsus2   Em(add9)

ev-'ry night   you   stay,   I'll be watch-in' you.   Oh, can't you

𝄋 Bridge

Csus2   C7(no3rd)   Gadd9

see?   You be-long   to   me.   How my poor   heart

Aadd9   Dsus2

aches   with ev-'ry step   you   take.   2., 3. Ev-'ry move   you

*2/3CII

*See below.

Verse

w/ Verse pattern

Gadd9   Em(add9)

make,   and ev-'ry vow you   break,   ev-'ry smile   you   fake,

To Coda ⊕

Csus2   Dsus2   Em(add9)

ev-'ry claim   you   stake,   I'll be watch-in'   you.

Bridge

E♭   F

Since you've gone, I've been lost   with-out   a   trace.   I dream at night, I can on - ly see your face.

w/ Bridge pattern

E♭   F

I look a-round, but it's   you I   can't   re-place.   I feel so cold and I   long for your   em-brace.

E♭

I   keep   call -   in'   "Ba   -   by,   ba -   by,   please."

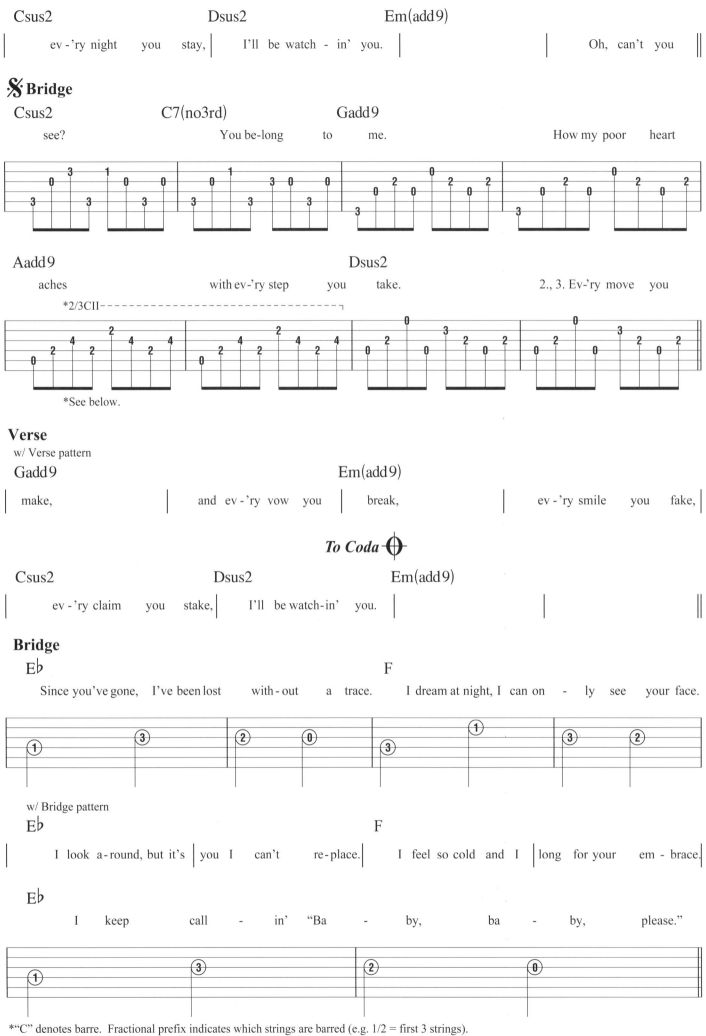

*"C" denotes barre. Fractional prefix indicates which strings are barred (e.g. 1/2 = first 3 strings).
  Roman numeral suffix indicates barred fret.

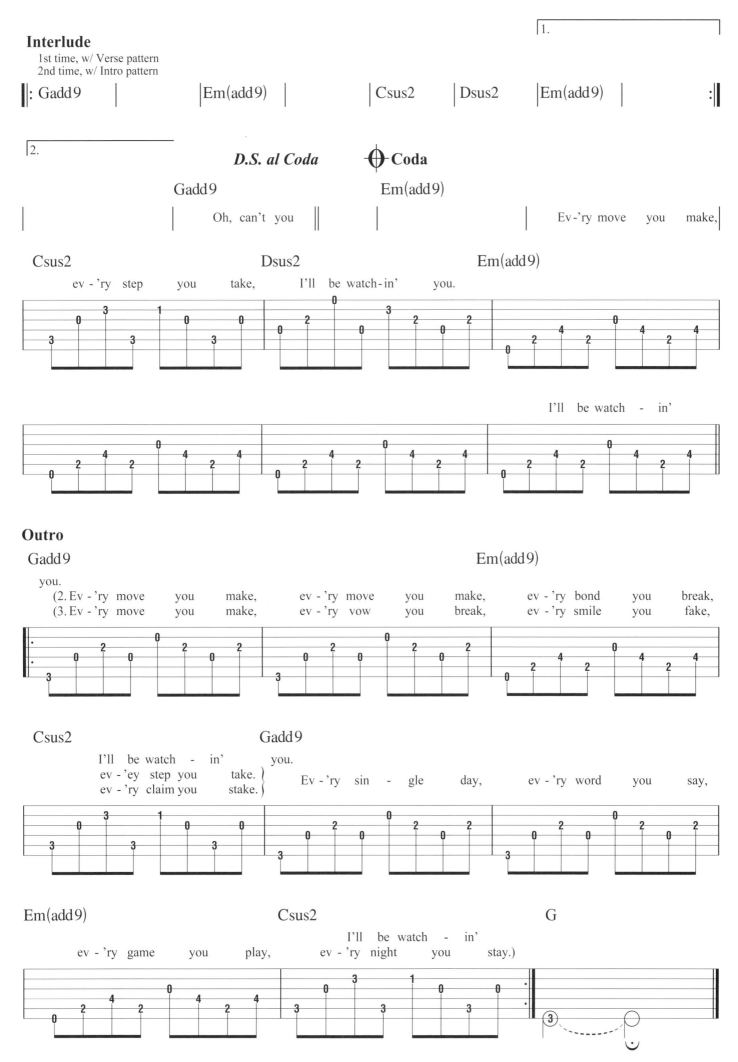

Dragonborn
(Skyrim Theme)

By Jeremy Soule

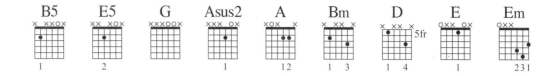

Key of Bm

Moderately slow

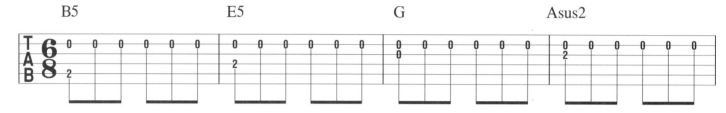

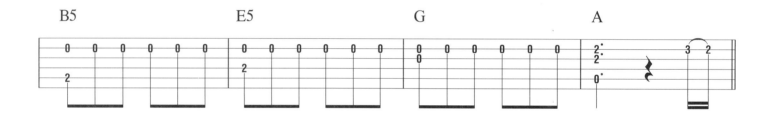

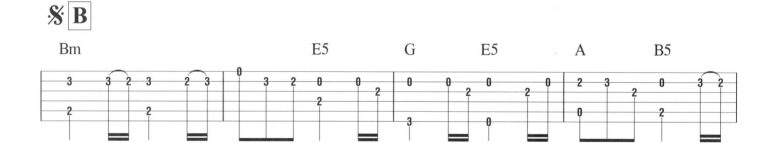

To Coda

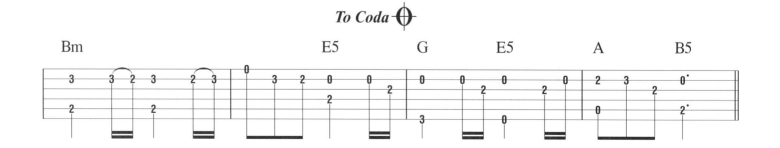

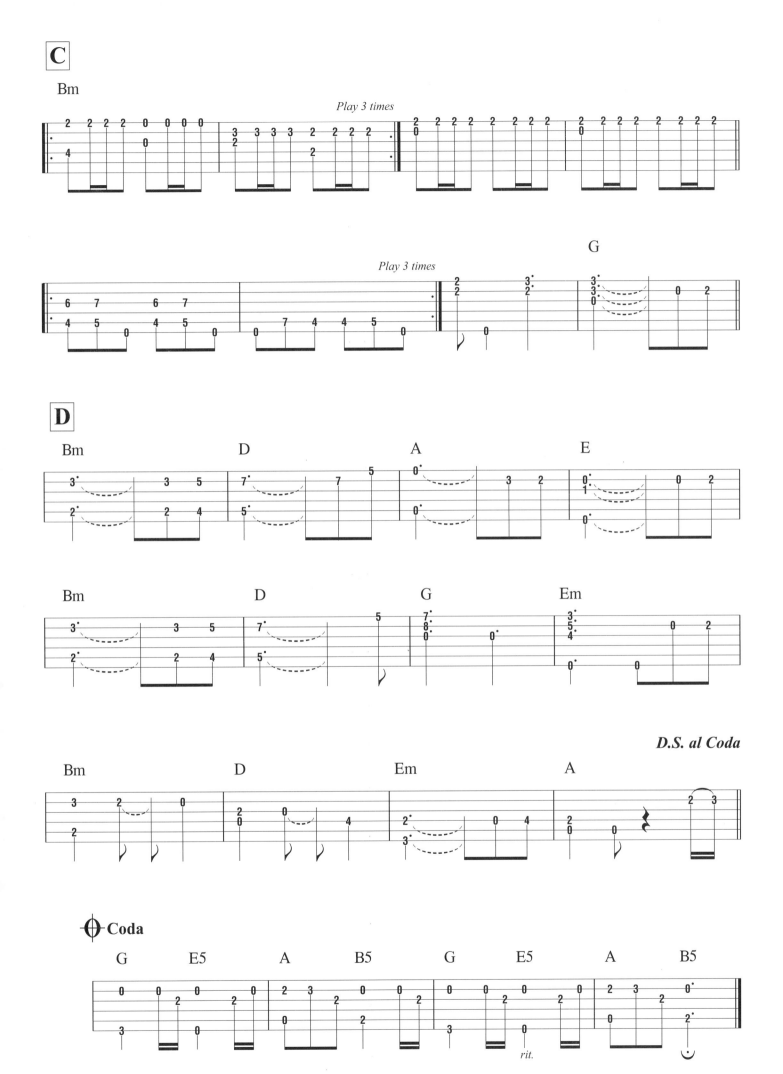

Everybody Hurts

Words and Music by William Berry, Peter Buck, Michael Mills and Michael Stipe

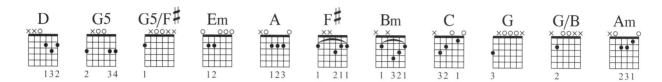

Key of D
Intro
Slow

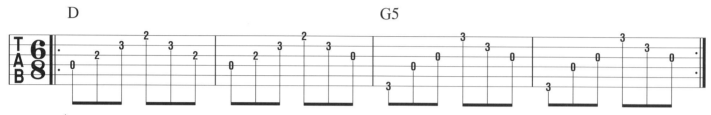

§ Verse

D   G5

etc.   1. When your day   is   long   and the night,
long.   2. When your day   is   night   a - lone,
             3. *See additional lyrics*   (Hold   on,   hold

D   G5

           the   night   is   yours   a - lone.
           if you   feel   like   let-tin' go,
on,   hold   on.)

D   G5

        When you're   sure you've   had   e - nough
        if   you   think you've   had   too   much   of this life,

To Coda ⊕

D   G5   G5/F♯

           well, hang on.

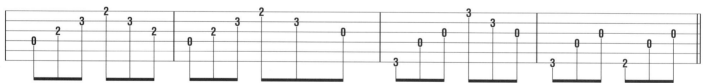

Chorus

Em   A

        Don't   let your - self   go,
        'Cause   ev - 'ry - bod-y   hurts.

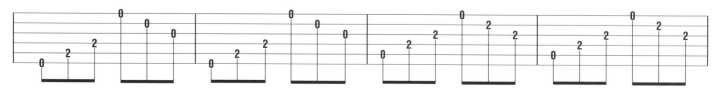

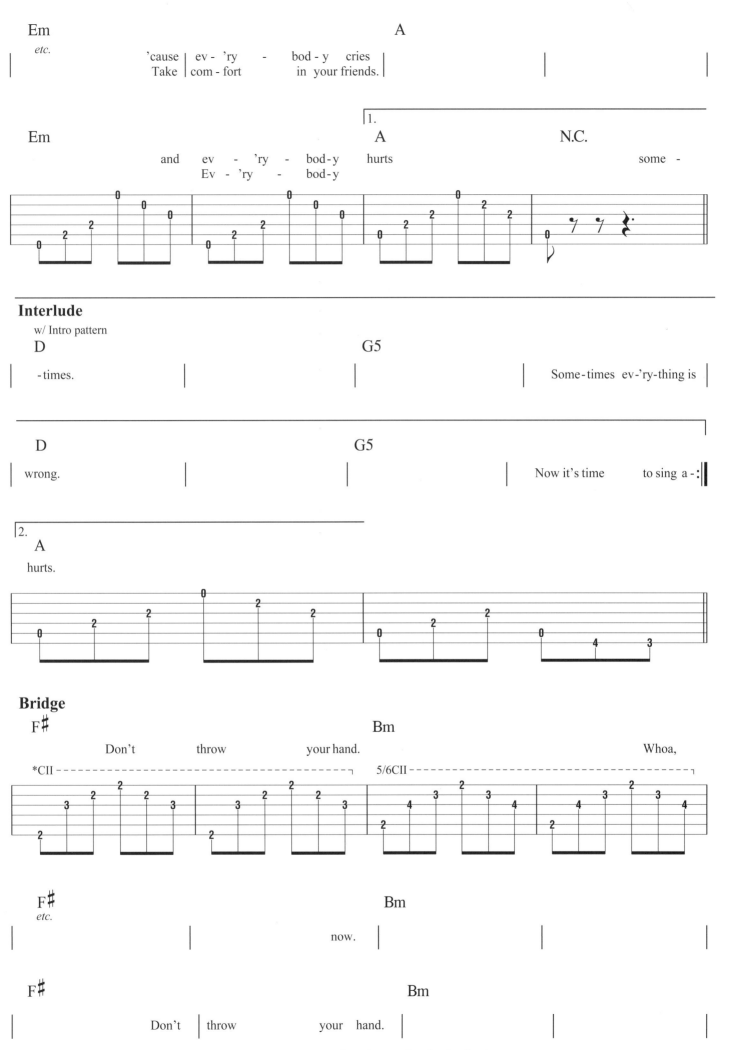

Interlude

w/ Intro pattern

Bridge

*"C" denotes barre. Fractional prefix indicates which strings are barred (e.g. 1.2 = first 3 strings).
Roman numeral suffix indicates barred fret.

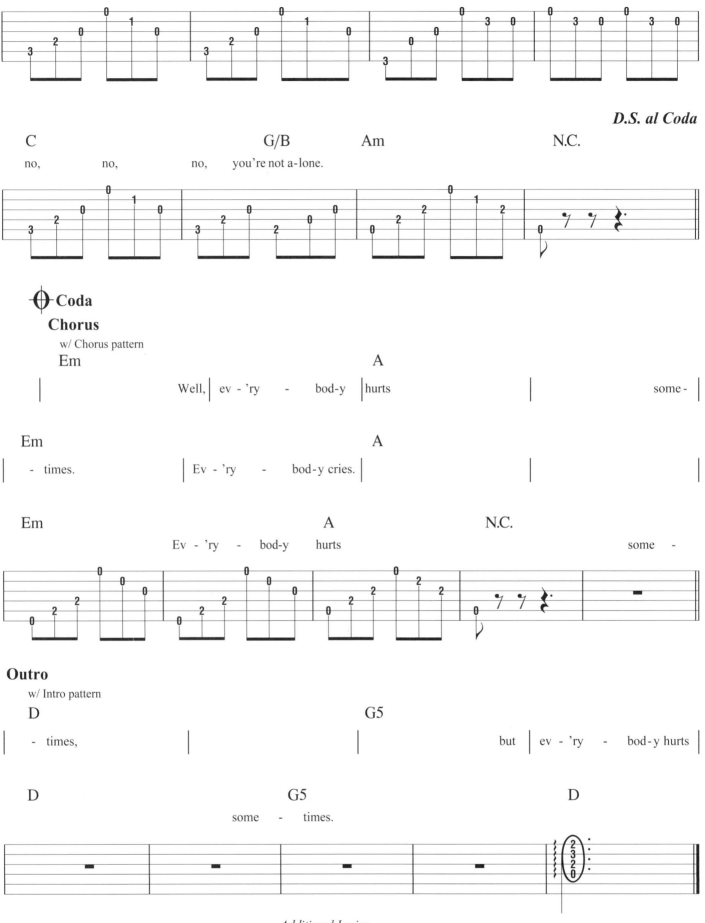

C   **G**

If you feel like you're a-lone,

D.S. al Coda

C   **G/B**   **Am**   **N.C.**

no,   no,   no,   you're not a-lone.

Coda

Chorus

w/ Chorus pattern

Em   **A**

Well, ev - 'ry - bod-y hurts   some -

Em   **A**

- times.   Ev - 'ry - bod-y cries.

Em   **A**   **N.C.**

Ev - 'ry - bod-y hurts   some -

Outro

w/ Intro pattern

D   **G5**

- times,   but ev - 'ry - bod-y hurts

D   **G5**   **D**

some - times.

Additional Lyrics

3. If you're on your own in this life,
   The days and nights are long.
   When you think you've had too much
   Of this life to hang on.

The 59th Street Bridge Song
(Feelin' Groovy)

Words and Music by Paul Simon

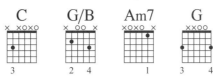

Capo V
Key of C (Capo Key of G)
Intro
Moderately

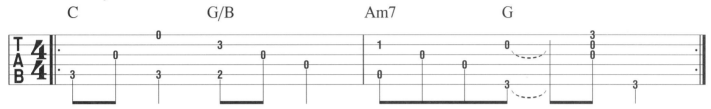

Verse

| C | G/B | Am7 | G | C | G/B |

etc.

1. Slow down,   you move too fast.   You got to make the morn-
2. Hel - lo, lamp - post.   What - cha know-in'?   I've come to watch your flow-
(3.) deeds to do, no prom - is - es to keep.   I'm dap - pled and drow - sy and

| Am7 | G | C | G/B | Am7 | G |

- in' last.   Just kick-in' down the cob - ble - stones,
- ers grow - in'.   Ain't you got no rhymes for me?
read - y to sleep, let the morn - ing - time drop all it's pet - als on me.

| C | G/B | Am7 | G | C | G/B |

look - in' for fun and feel - in' groov - y.
Do, do, do, do, do, feel - in' groov - y.
Life, I love you. All is groov - y.

| Am7 | G | C | G/B | Am7 | G |

Ba, da, da, da, da, da, da.   Feel - in' groov - y.

1., 2.

| C | G/B | Am7 | G |

3. I got no

3.

| C | G/B | Am7 | G |

Ba, da, da, da, da, da, dum.

rit.

Für Elise, WoO 59

By Ludwig van Beethoven

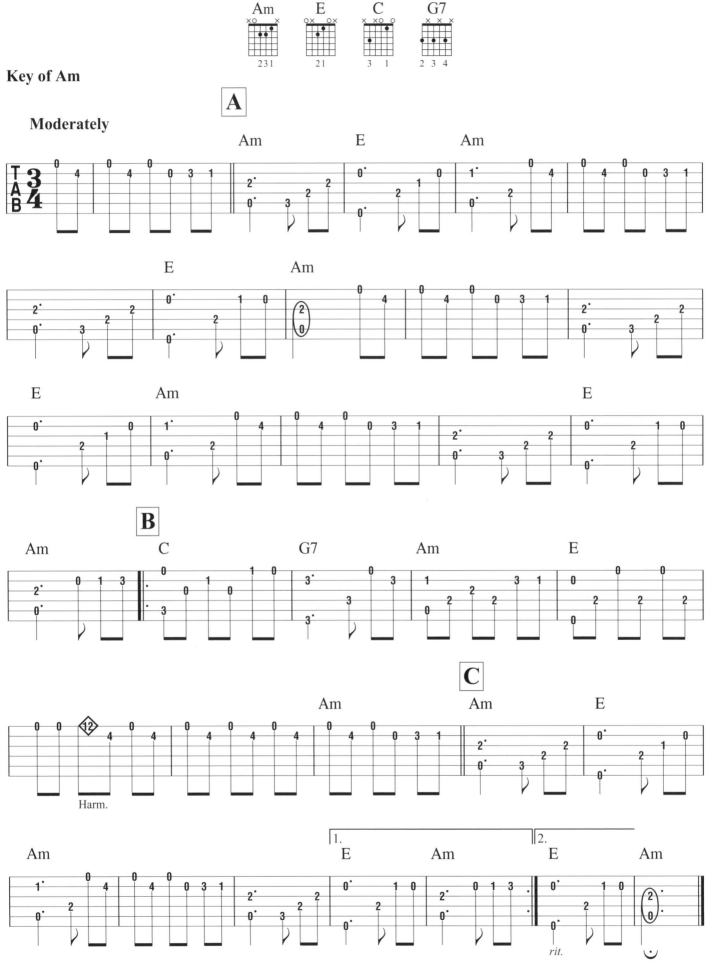

Happy Birthday to You

Words and Music by Mildred J. Hill and Patty S. Hill

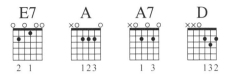

Key of A
Moderately

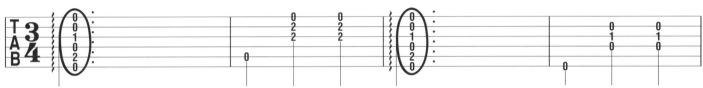

Game of Thrones

Theme from the HBO Series GAME OF THRONES

By Ramin Djawadi

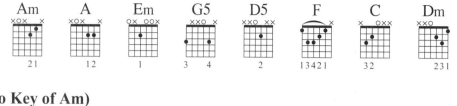

Capo III
Key of Cm (Capo Key of Am)

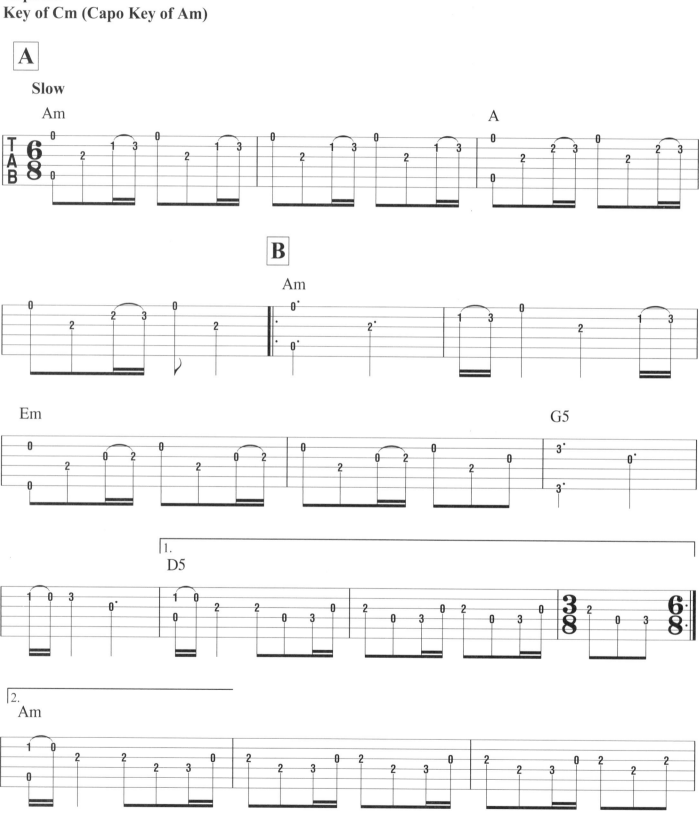

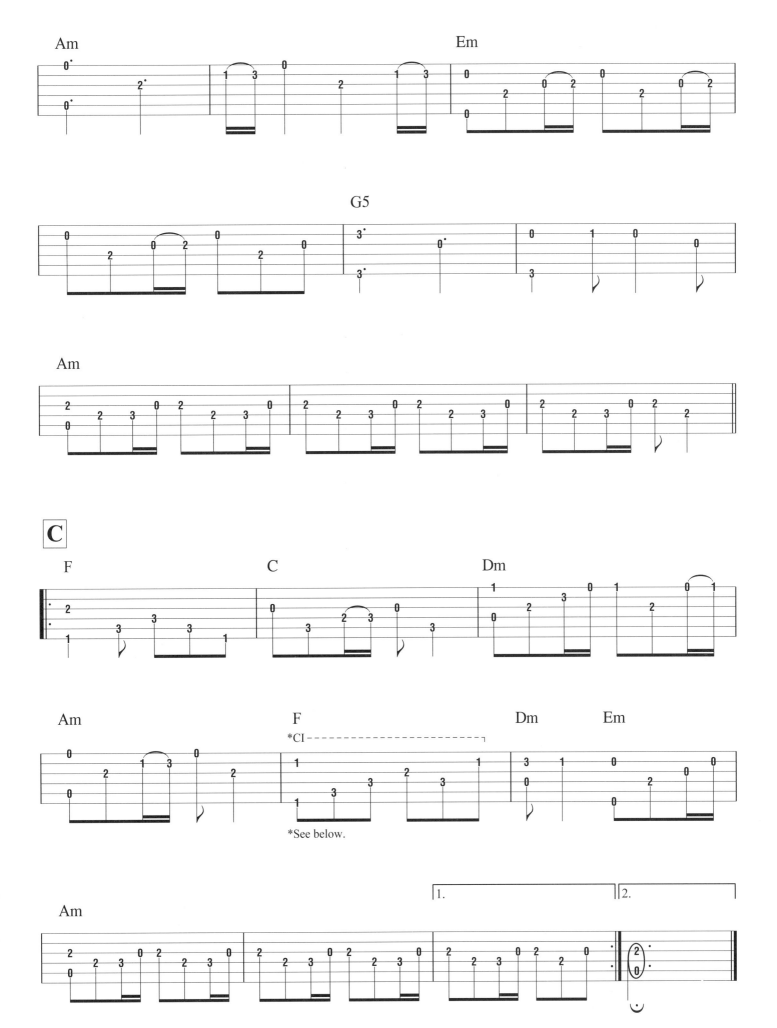

*"C" denotes barre. Fractional prefix indicates which strings are barred (e.g. 1/2 = first 3 strings).
  Roman numeral suffix indicates barred fret.

God Only Knows

Words and Music by Brian Wilson and Tony Asher

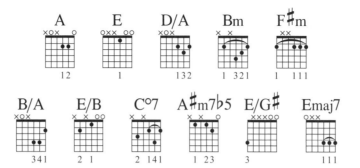

A   E   D/A   Bm   F♯m

B/A   E/B   C°7   A♯m7♭5   E/G♯   Emaj7

Key of E
Intro
Moderately (♪♪ = ♪♪)

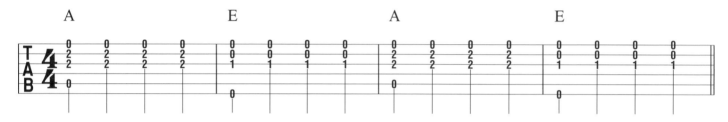

A   E   A   E

Verse

D/A   Bm   F♯m

1. I may not al-ways love you,   but long as there are
2. If you should ev-er leave me,   though life would still go

*5/6CII- - - - - - - - - - - - - - - - - - -   CII- - - - - - - - - - - - - - - - - - -

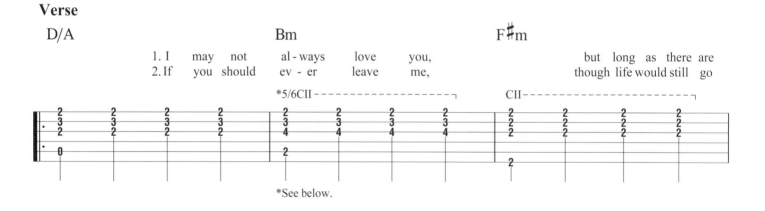

*See below.

B/A   E/B   C°7

stars a-bove you,   you nev-er need to doubt it.
on, be-lieve me,   the world could show noth-ing to me.

1/3CII- - - - - - - - - - - - - - - - - - -

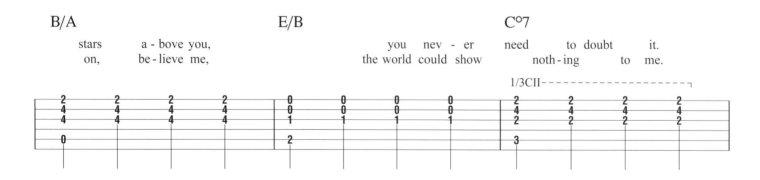

*"C" denotes barre. Fractional prefix indicates which strings are barred (e.g. 1/2 = first 3 strings).
  Roman numeral suffix indicates barred fret.

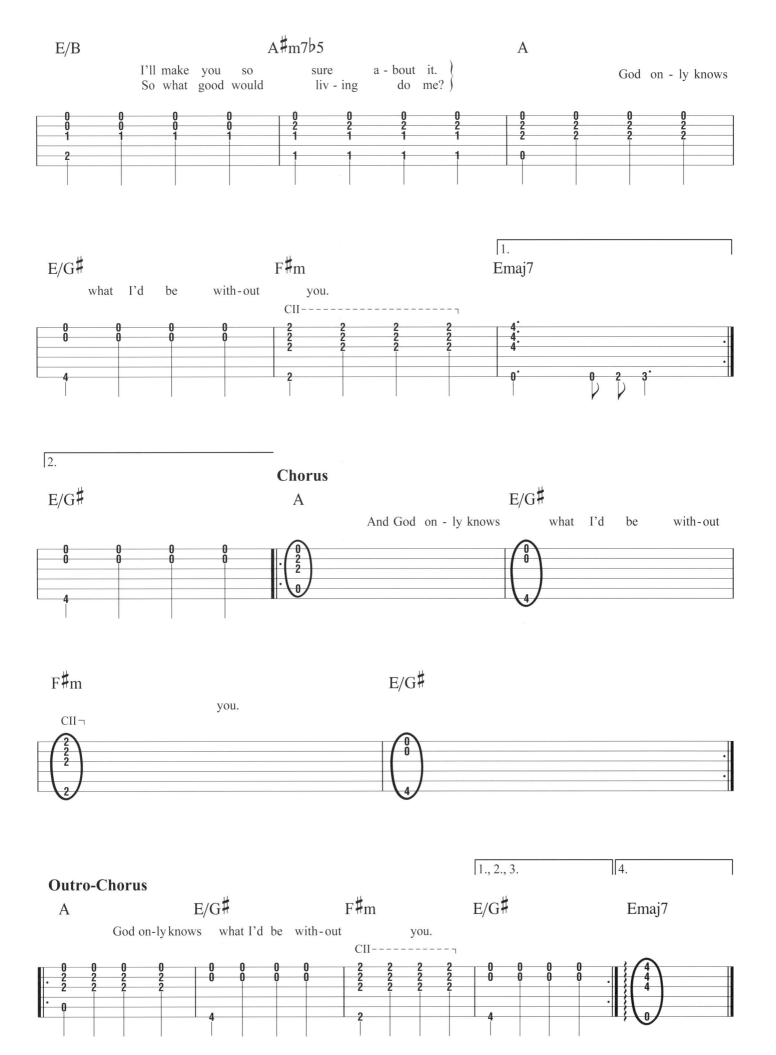

The Godfather
(Love Theme)

from the Paramount Picture THE GODFATHER

By Nino Rota

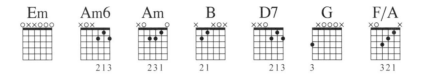

Capo VIII
Key of Cm (Capo Key of Em)

Slow

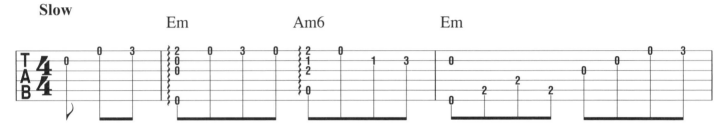

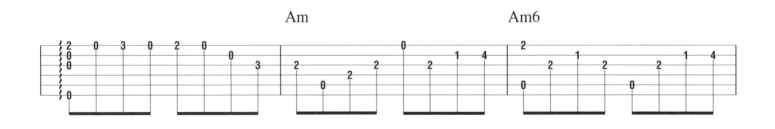

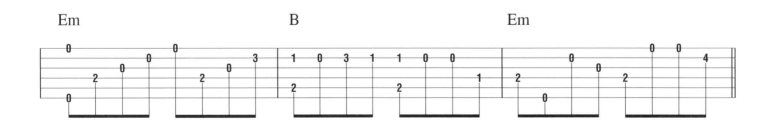

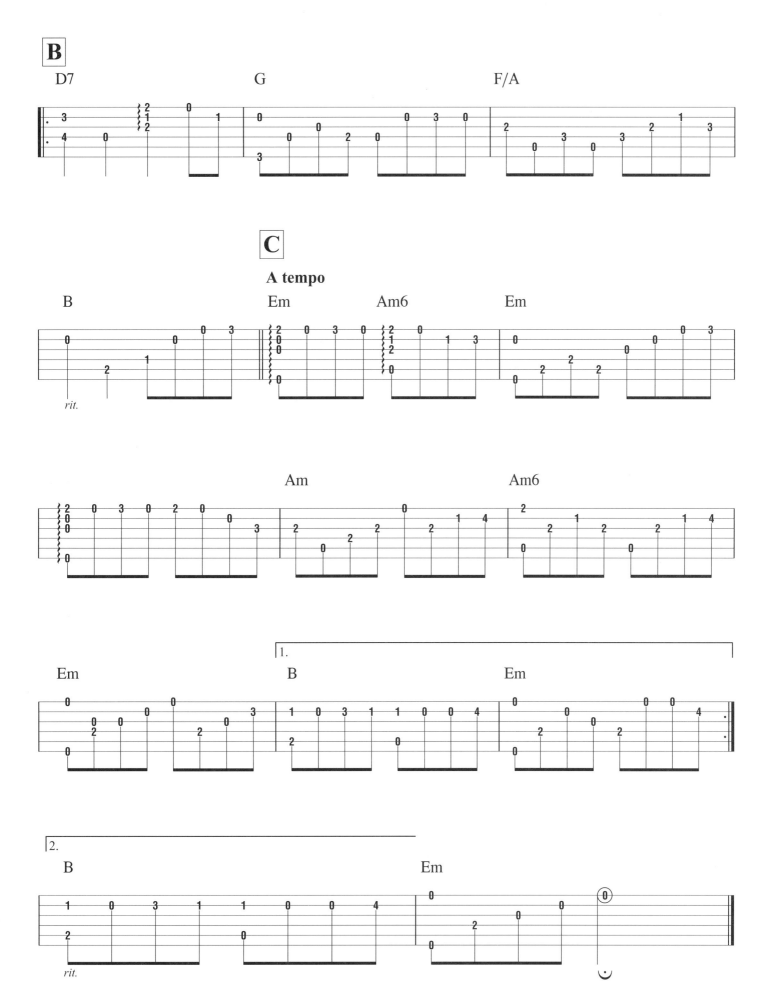

Good Riddance
(Time of Your Life)

Words by Billie Joe
Music by Green Day

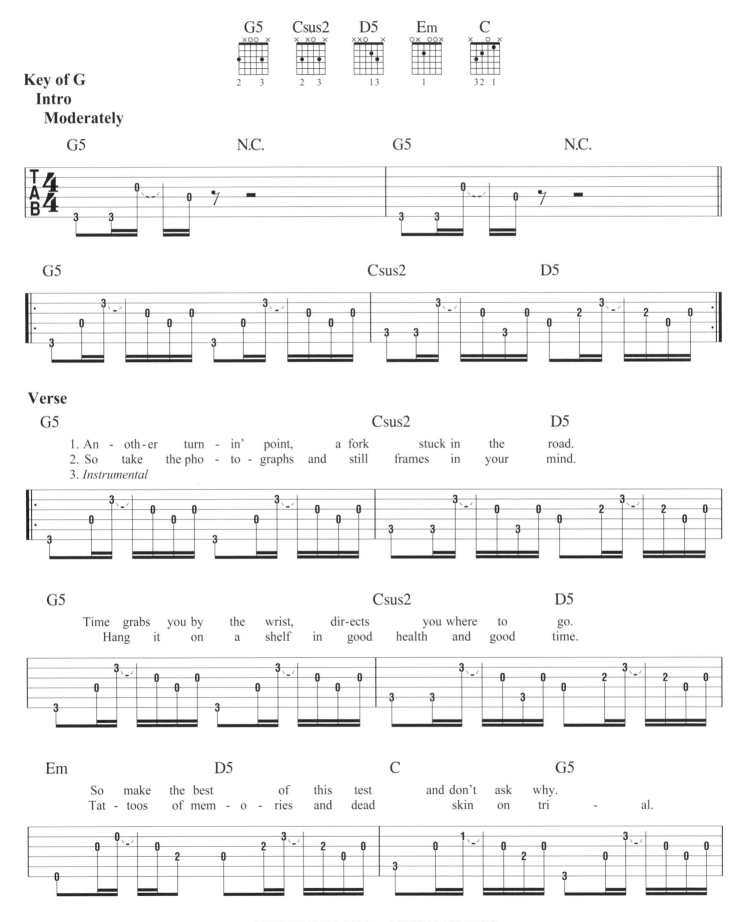

Key of G
Intro
Moderately

Verse

1. An-oth-er turn-in' point, a fork stuck in the road.
2. So take the pho-to-graphs and still frames in your mind.
3. *Instrumental*

Time grabs you by the wrist, dir-ects you where to go.
Hang it on a shelf in good health and good time.

So make the best of this test and don't ask why.
Tat-toos of mem-o-ries and dead skin on tri - al.

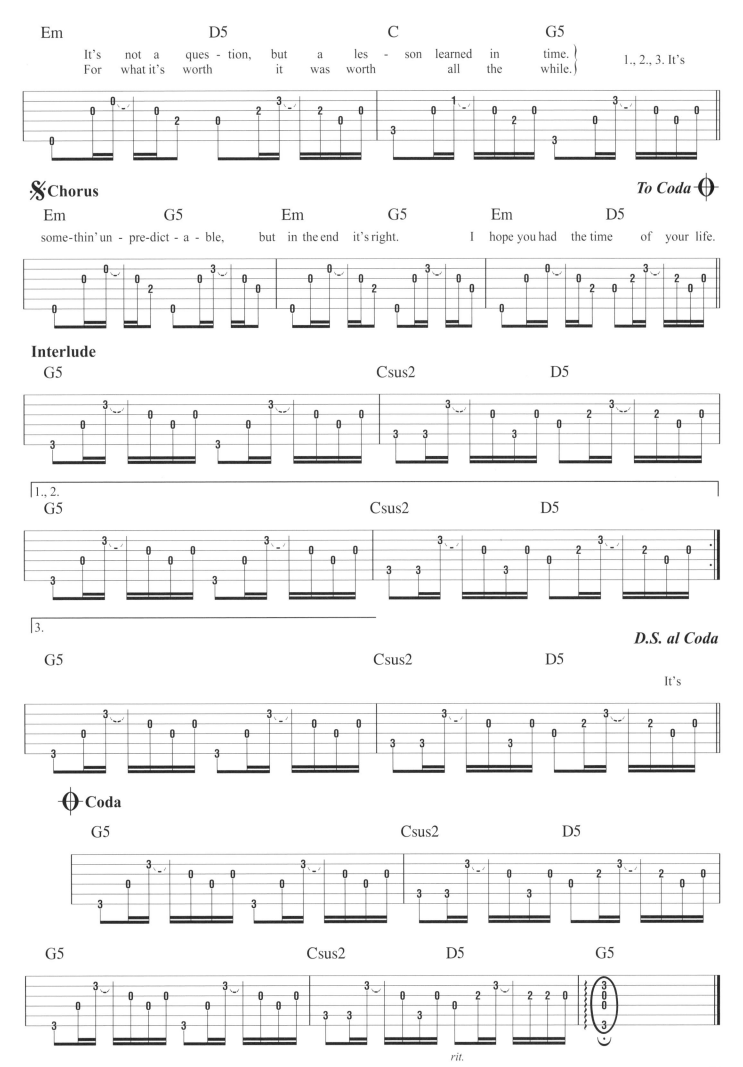

Chorus

Interlude

1., 2.

3.

D.S. al Coda

Coda

rit.

The House of the Rising Sun

Words and Music by Alan Price

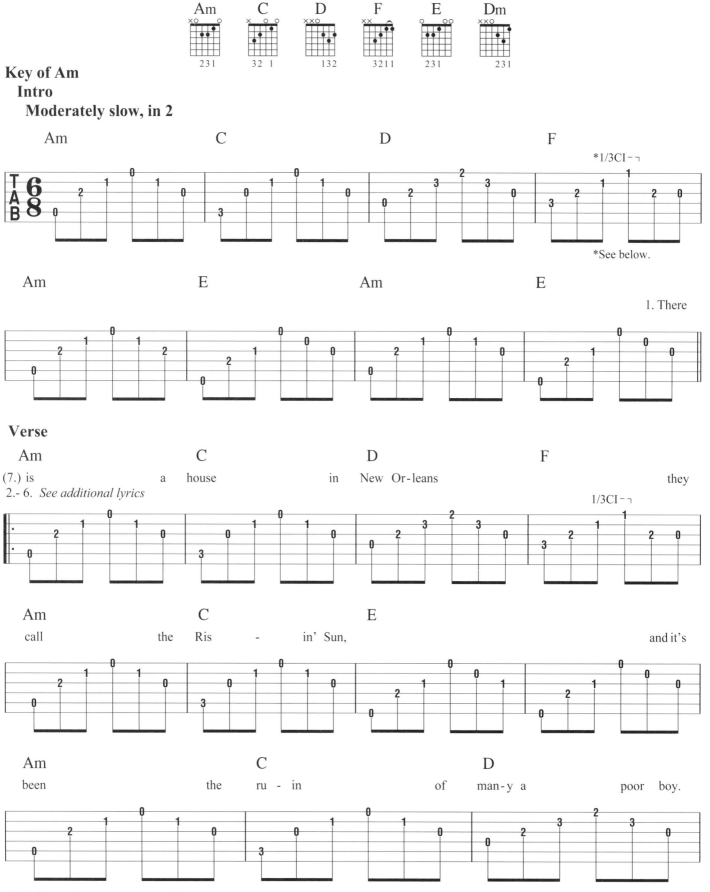

Key of Am
Intro
   Moderately slow, in 2

*“C” denotes barre. Fractional prefix indicates which strings are barred (e.g. 1/2 = first 3 strings).
   Roman numeral suffix indicates barred fret.

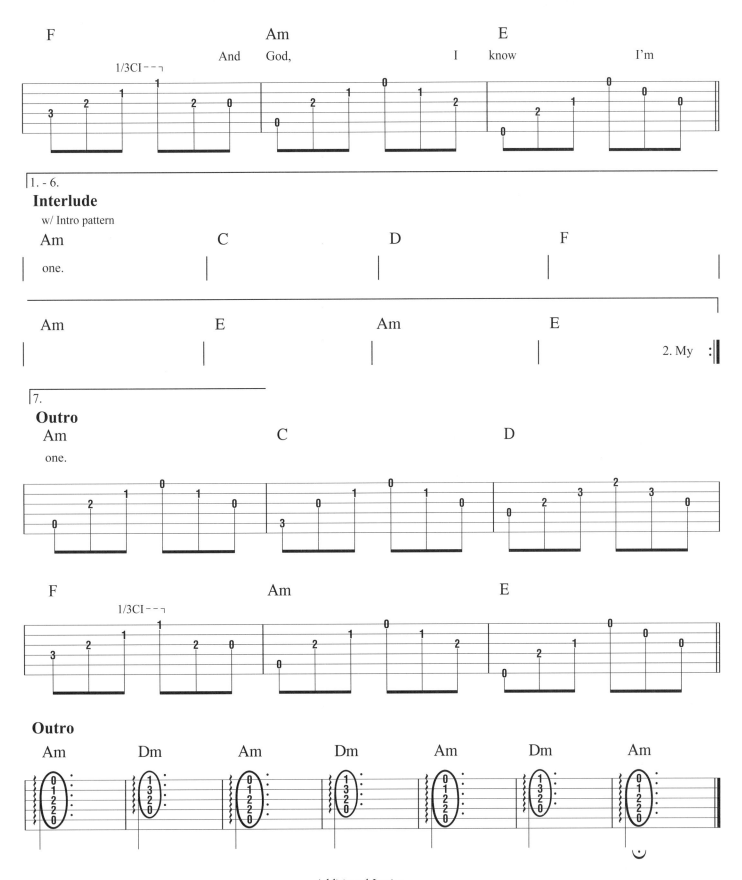

Additional Lyrics

2. My mother was a tailor
   She sewed my new blue jeans.
   My father was a gamblin' man
   Down in New Orleans.

3. Now, the only thing a gambler needs
   Is a suitcase and a trunk,
   And the only time he's satisfied
   Is when he's on a drunk.

4. *Instrumental*

5. Oh mother, tell your children
   Not to do what I have done.
   Spend your lives in sin and misery,
   In the House of the Rising Sun.

6. Well, I got one foot on the platform,
   The other foot on the train,
   I'm goin' back to New Orleans
   To wear that ball and chain.

Imagine

Words and Music by John Lennon

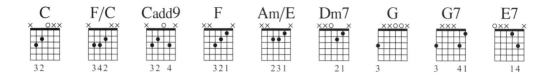

Key of C
Intro
Moderately slow

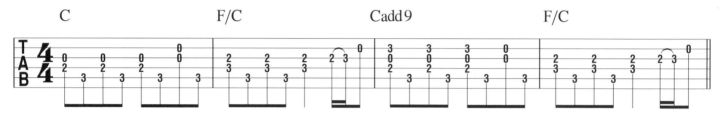

 Verse

Cadd9   F/C

1. Im-ag-ine   there's   no   heav-en.
   2. Im-ag-ine there's   no   coun - tries.
3. *See additional lyrics*

Cadd9   F/C

It's eas - y   if   you   try.
It is-n't hard   to   do.

Cadd9   F/C

No   hell   be - low us,
Noth-ing to kill   or   die   for,

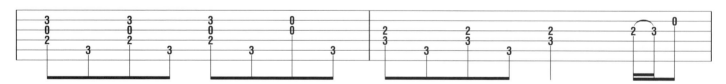

Cadd9   **F/C**

a-bove us   on - ly   sky.
and no re - li - gion,   too.

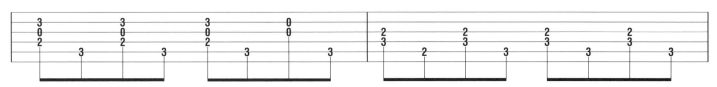

F   **Am/E**   **Dm7**   **F/C**

Im - ag - ine all   the   peo - ple
Im - ag - ine all   the   peo - ple

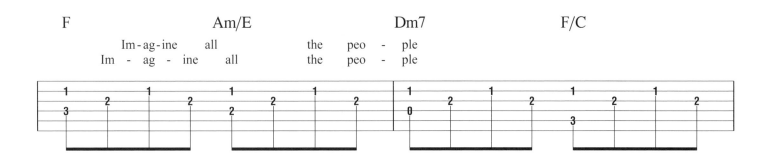

G   **G7**

liv - in'   for   to - day,   ah,   ah.
liv - in'   life   in peace.   You,

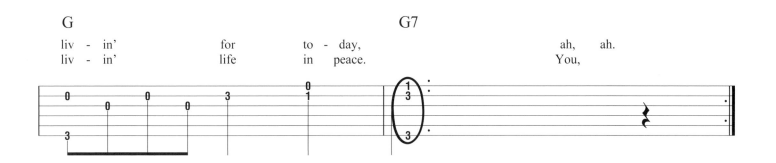

Chorus

F   **G**   **Cadd9**   **E7**

you   may say   I'm a dream - er,

F   **G**   **Cadd9**   **E7**

but I'm   not   the on - ly one.

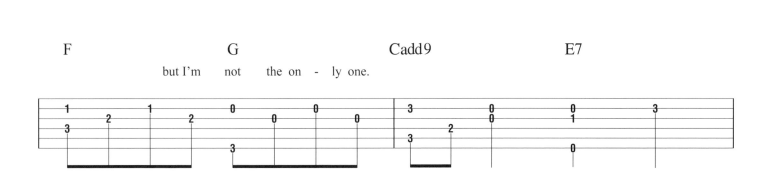

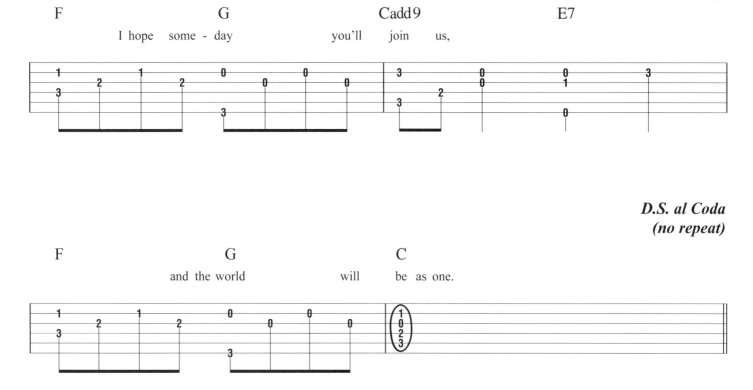

**D.S. al Coda
(no repeat)**

⊕ **Coda**

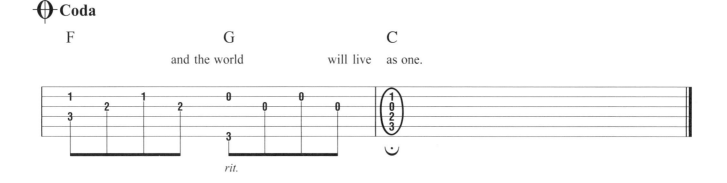

rit.

Additional Lyrics

3. Imagine no possessions.
   I wonder if you can.
   No need for greed or hunger,
   A brotherhood of man.
   Imagine all the people sharing all the world.
   You...

Minuet in G

from THE ANNA MAGDALENA NOTEBOOK (originally for keyboard)

By Johann Sebastian Bach

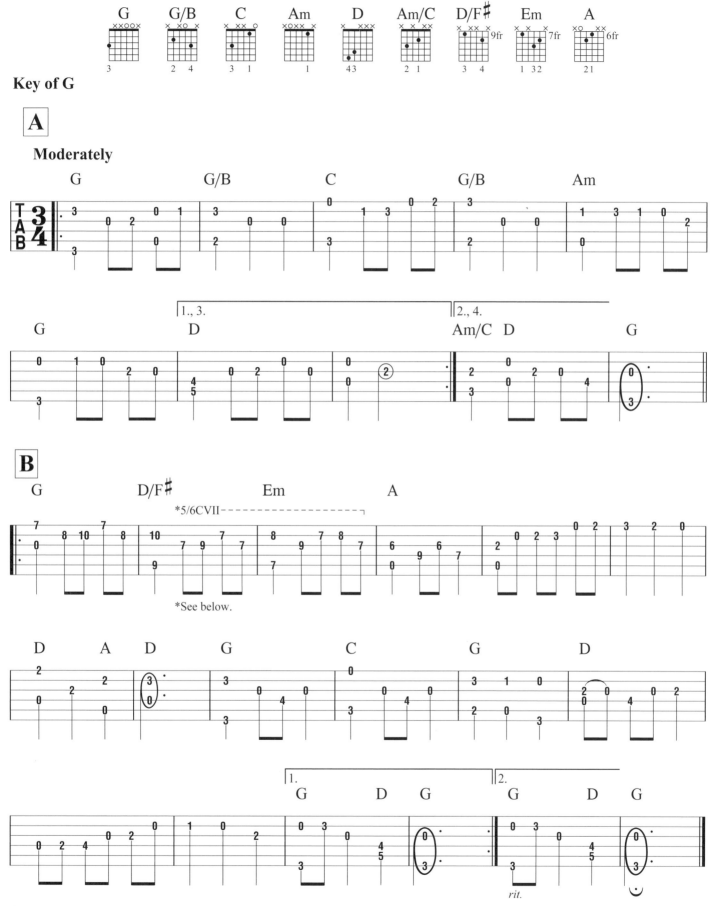

*"C" denotes barre. Fractional prefix indicates which strings are barred (e.g. 1/2 = first 3 strings). Roman numeral suffix indicates barred fret.

In My Life

Words and Music by John Lennon and Paul McCartney

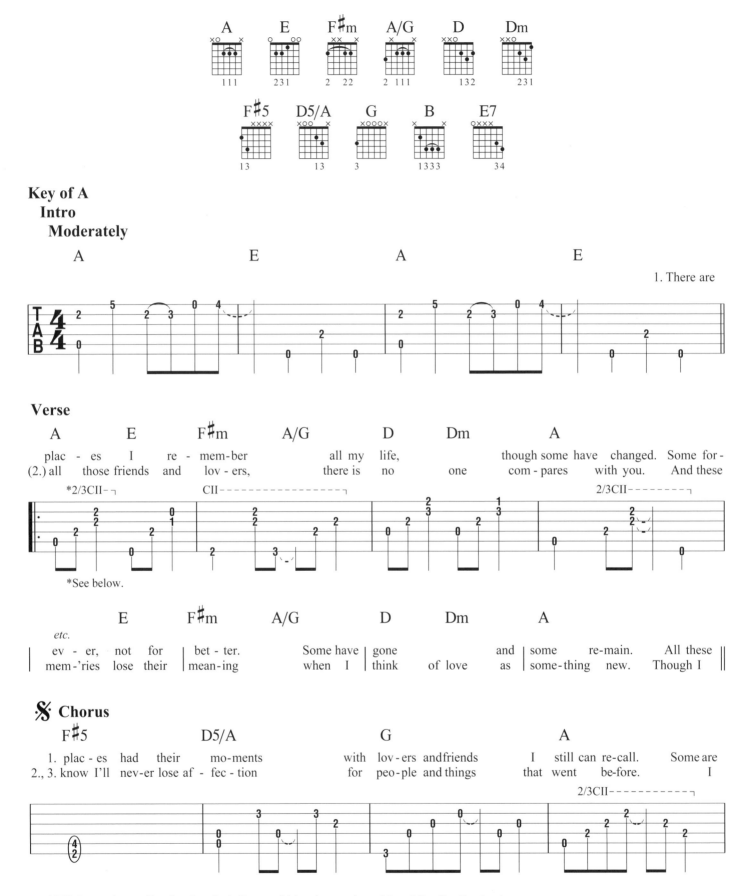

Key of A
Intro
Moderately

1. There are

Verse

plac - es I re - mem - ber all my life, though some have changed. Some for-
(2.) all those friends and lov - ers, there is no one com - pares with you. And these

*See below.

ev - er, not for bet - ter. Some have gone and some re - main. All these
mem - 'ries lose their mean - ing when I think of love as some - thing new. Though I

Chorus

1. plac - es had their mo - ments with lov - ers and friends I still can re - call. Some are
2., 3. know I'll nev - er lose af - fec - tion for peo - ple and things that went be - fore. I

*"C" denotes barre. Fractional prefix indicates which strings are barred (e.g. 1/2 = first 3 strings).
Roman numeral suffix indicates barred fret.

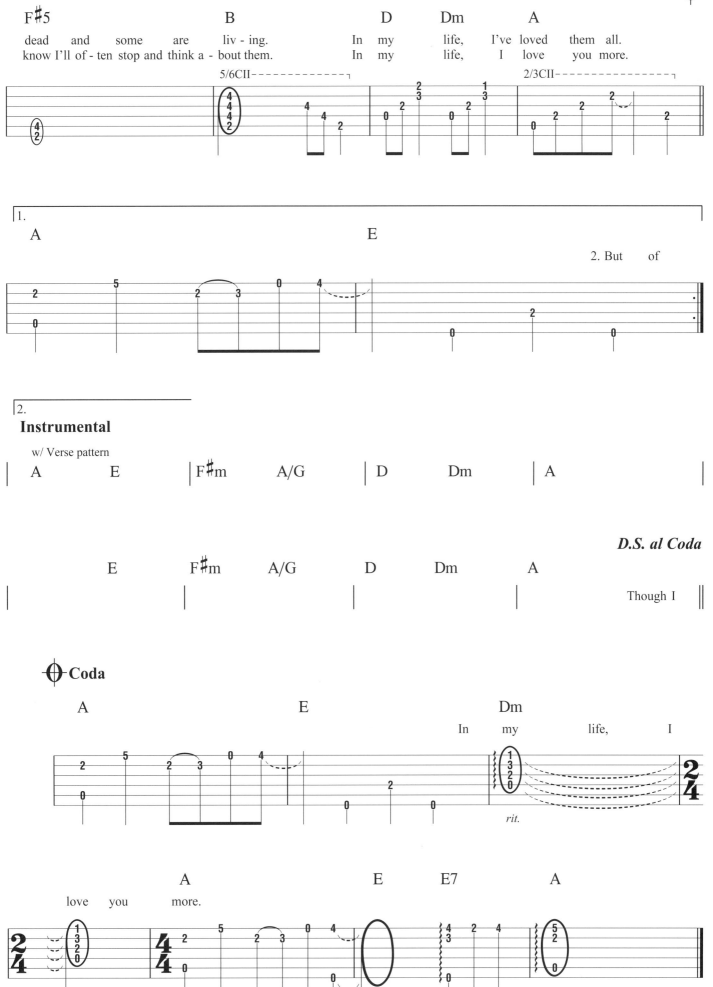

Key to the Highway

Words and Music by William Lee Conley Broonzy and Chas. Segar

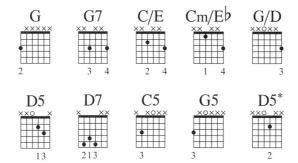

Key of G

Intro

Moderately slow (♩♩ = ♩♪)

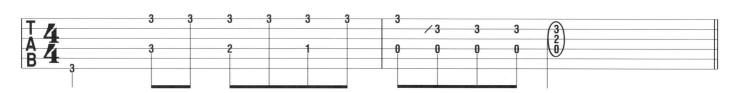

1. I've got the

Verse

key

to the high-way,

2. - 6. *See additional lyrics*

billed out and bound to go. I'm gon-na leave

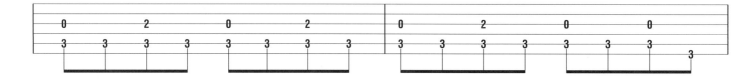

G5   **D5***

here   run-nin' be-cause   walk - in's   most   too   slow.

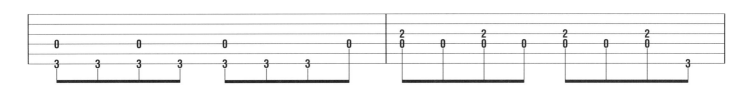

1. - 5.

G   **D7**

2. I'm   go - in' back

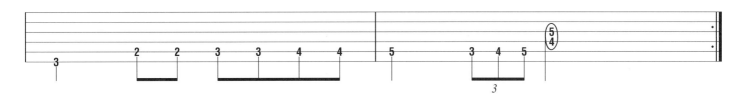

6.

G

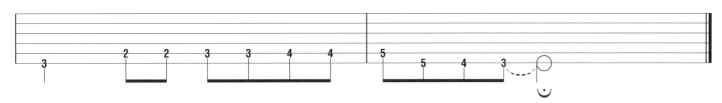

Additional Lyrics

2. I'm goin' back to the border
   Where I'm better known
   Because you haven't done nothin'
   But drove a good man away from home.

3. Give me one more kiss, mama,
   Just before I go
   'Cause when I leave this time, girl,
   I won't be back no more.

4. *Instrumental*

5. When the moon peeps over the mountain,
   Honey, I'll be on my way.
   I'm gonna roam this highway
   Until the break of day.

6. Well, it's so long, so long, babe.
   I must say goodbye.
   I'm gonna roam this highway
   Until the day I die.

Lean on Me

Words and Music by Bill Withers

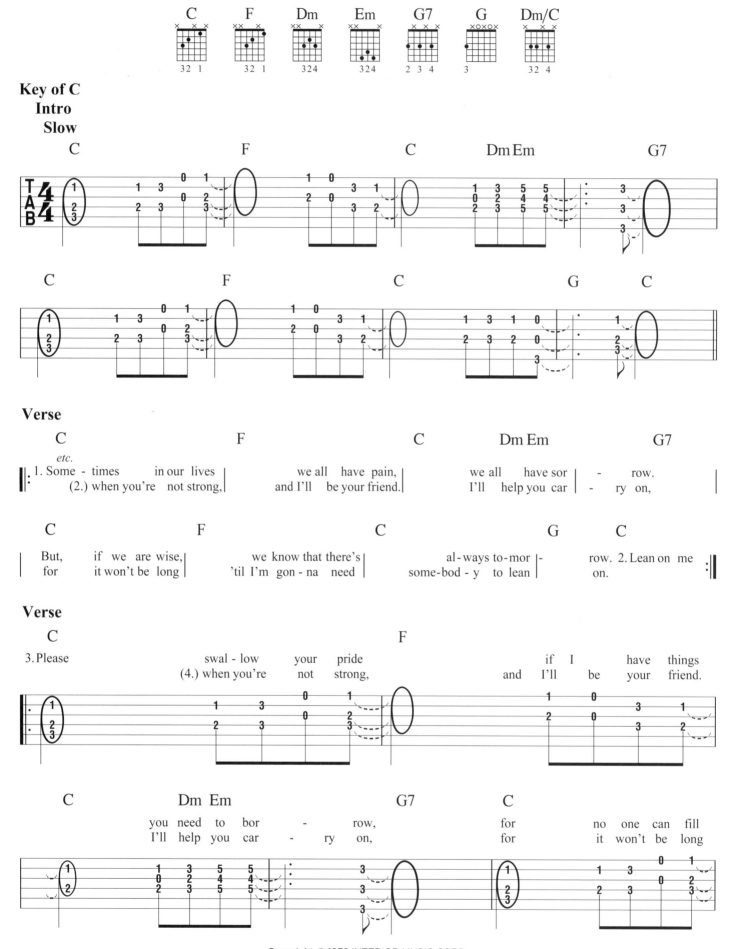

48

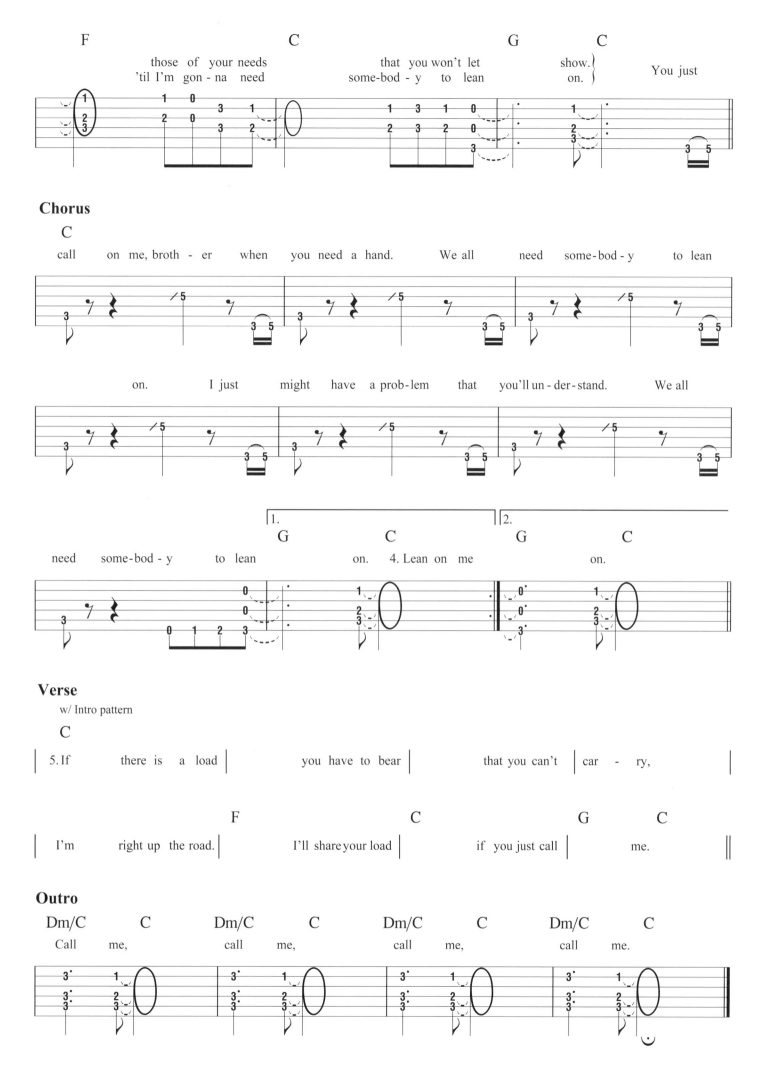

Chorus

Verse

w/ Intro pattern

Outro

Listen to Your Heart

Words and Music by Per Gessle and Mats Persson

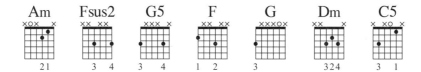

Capo II
Key of Bm (Capo Key of Am)
Intro
Moderately slow

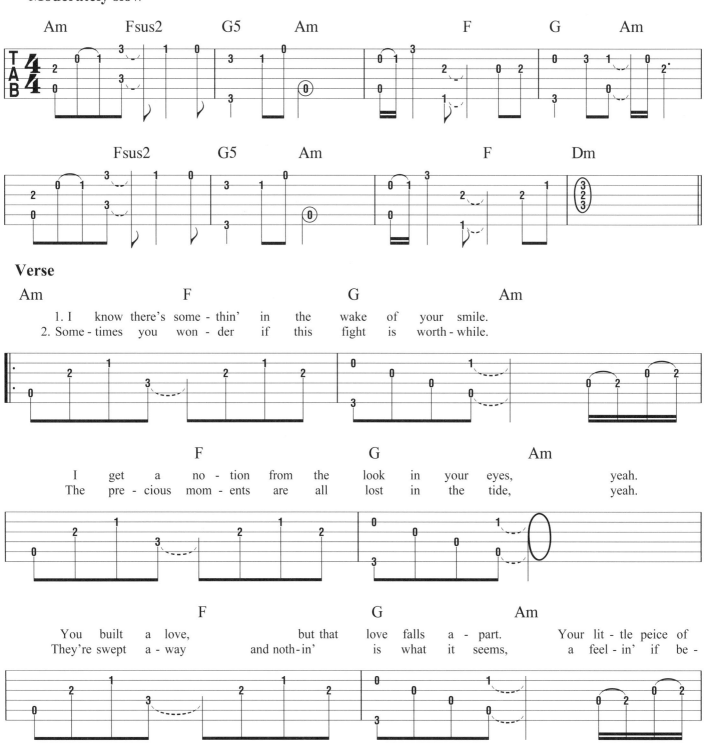

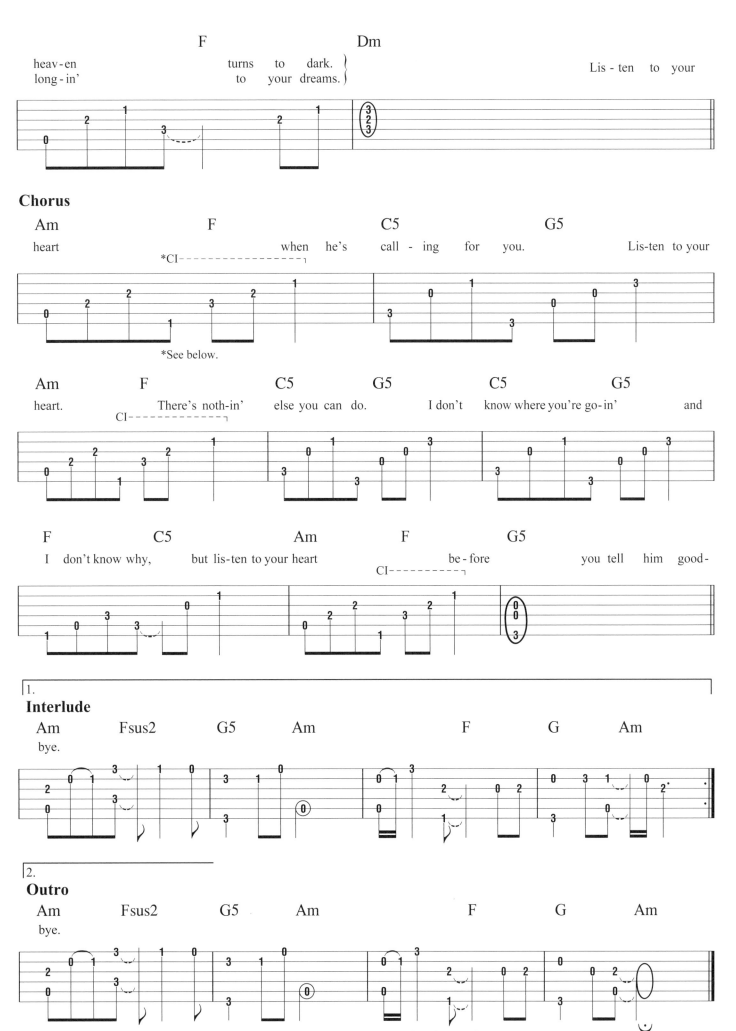

Chorus

Interlude

Outro

*"C" denotes barre. Fractional prefix indicates which strings are barred (e.g. 1/2 = first 3 strings).
Roman numeral suffix indicates barred fret.

Moon River

from the Paramount Picture BREAKFAST AT TIFFANY'S
Words by Johnny Mercer
Music by Henry Mancini

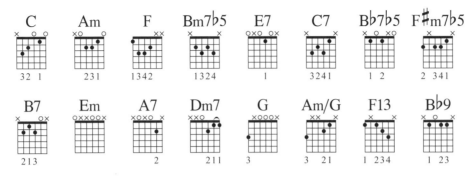

Key of C

Intro

Moderately slow

Verse

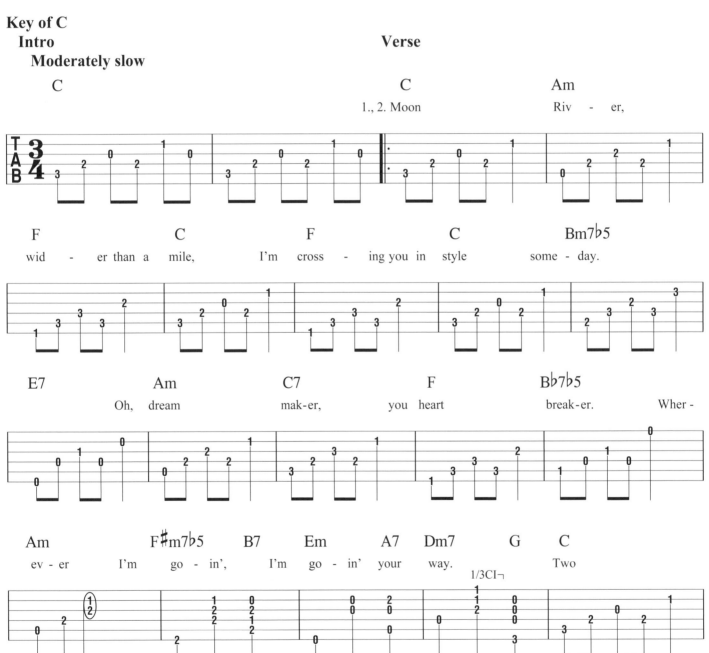

*"C" denotes barre. Fractional prefix indicates which strings are barred (e.g. 1/2 = first 3 strings).
Roman numeral suffix indicates barred fret.

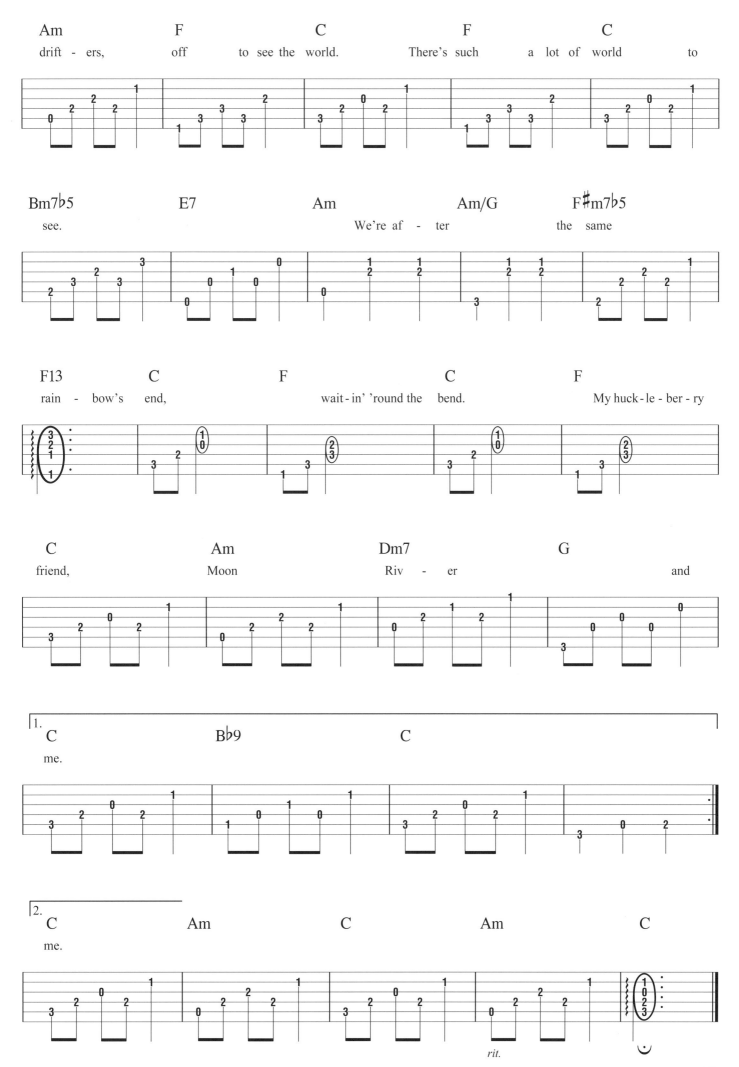

No Woman No Cry

Words and Music by Vincent Ford

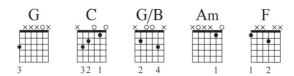

Key of C
Intro
Moderately slow

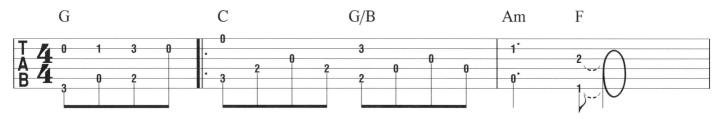

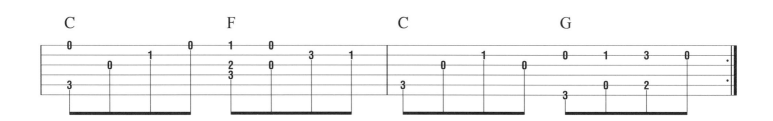

Chorus
w/ Intro pattern

C	G/B	Am	F	C	F	C	G		C	G

‖: No wom-an, no | cry. | | No wom-an, no cry. | :‖ 1. Said, said,

Verse

C   G/B   Am   F

said I re-mem-ber   when we used   to   sit

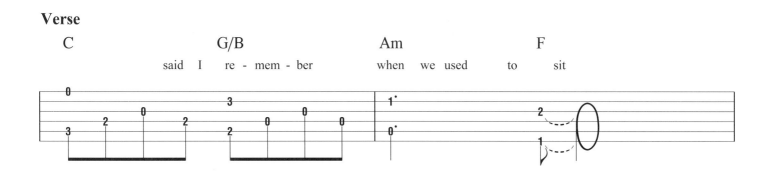

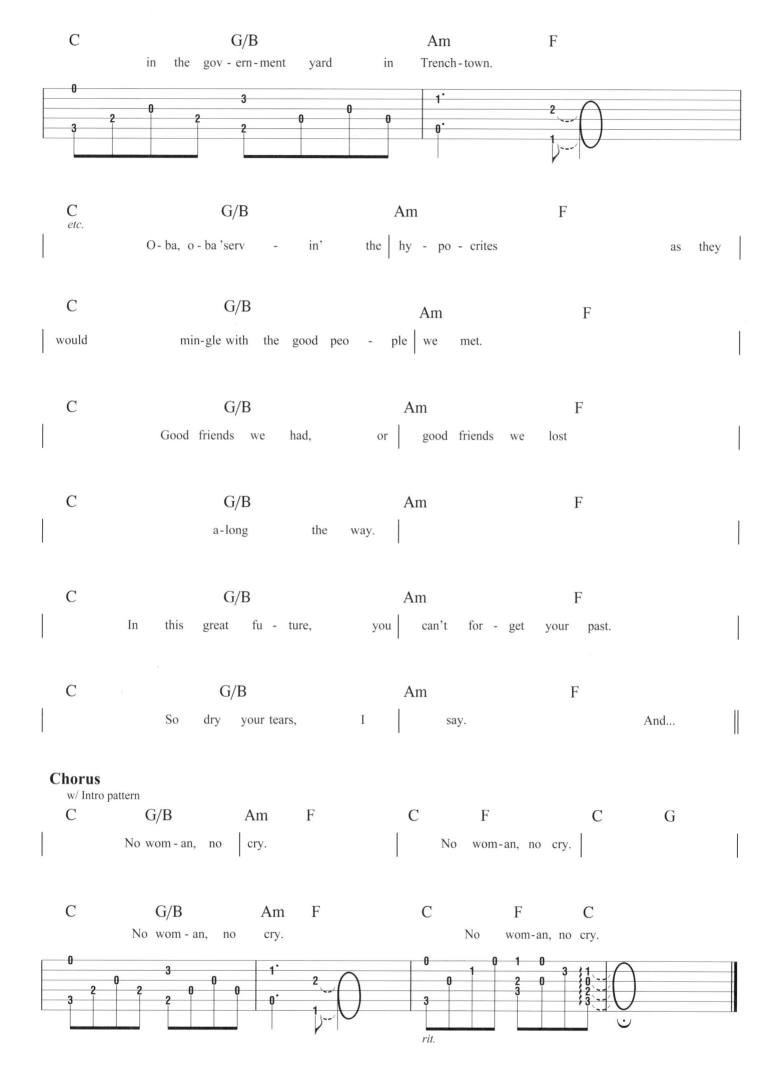

Chorus

w/ Intro pattern

Nothing Else Matters

Words and Music by James Hetfield and Lars Ulrich

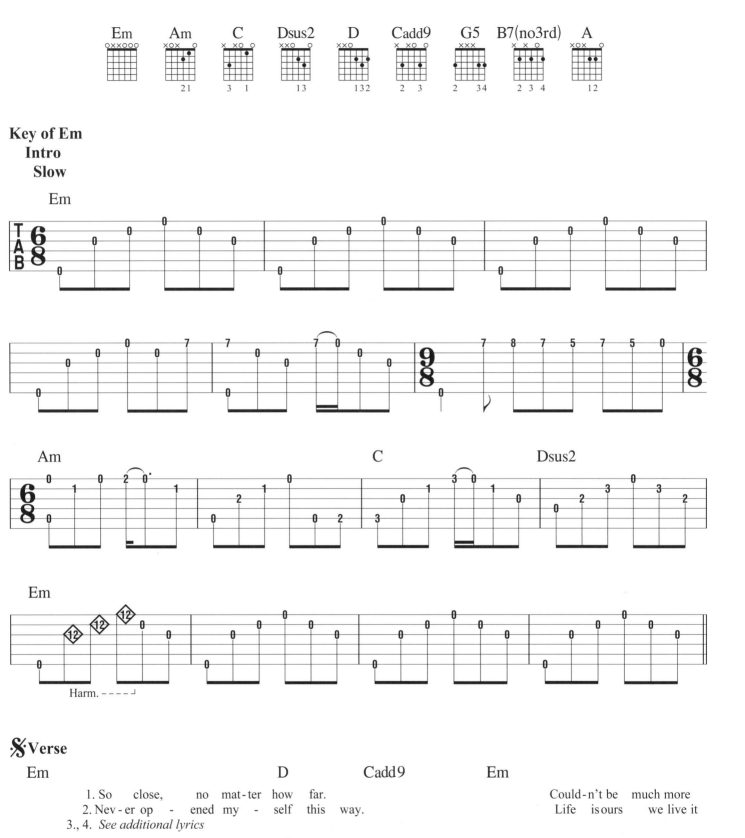

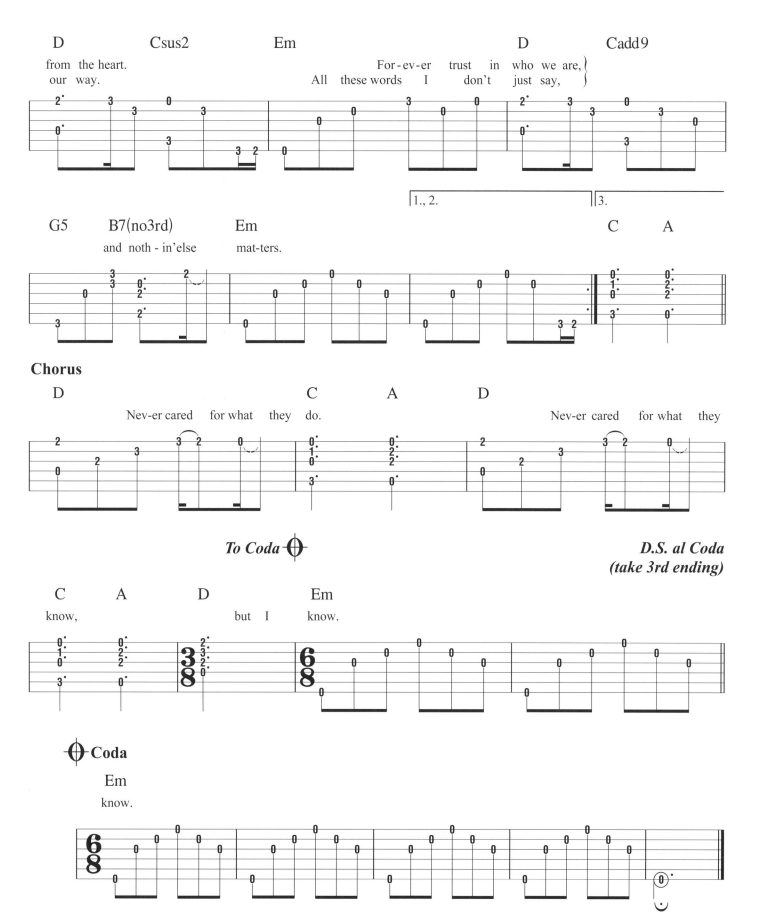

Additional Lyrics

3. Trust I seek and I find in you.
Every day for us, something new.
Open mind for a different view,
And nothing else matters.

4. So close, no matter how far.
I couldn't be much more from the heart.
Forever trust in who we are,
And nothing else matters.

Over the Rainbow

from THE WIZARD OF OZ

Music by Harold Arlen

Lyric by E.Y. "Yip" Harburg

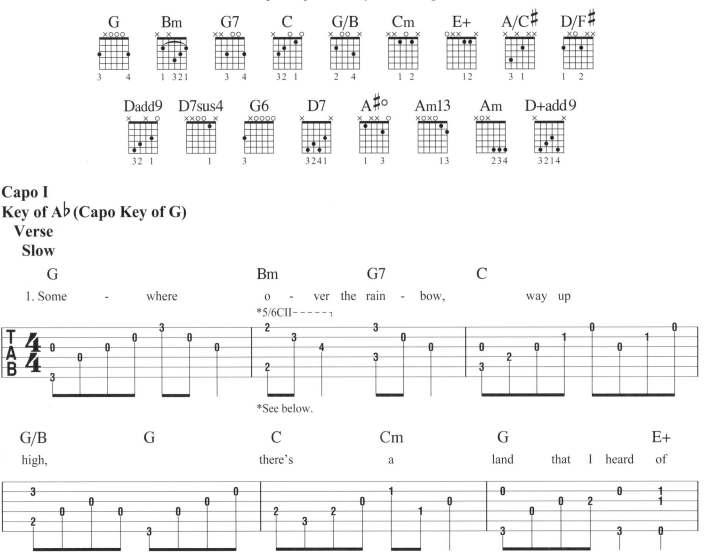

Capo I

Key of A♭ (Capo Key of G)

Verse

Slow

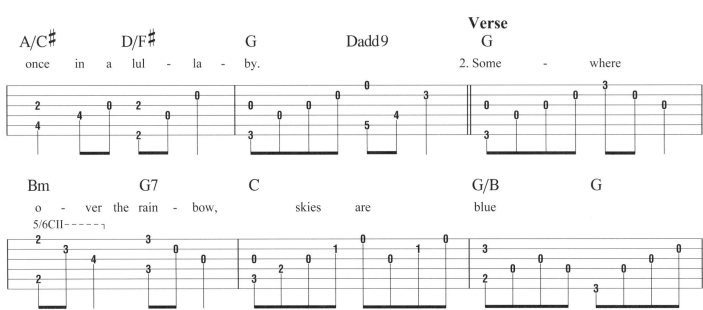

*"C" denotes barre. Fractional prefix indicates which strings are barred (e.g. 1/2 = first 3 strings).
Roman numeral suffix indicates barred fret.

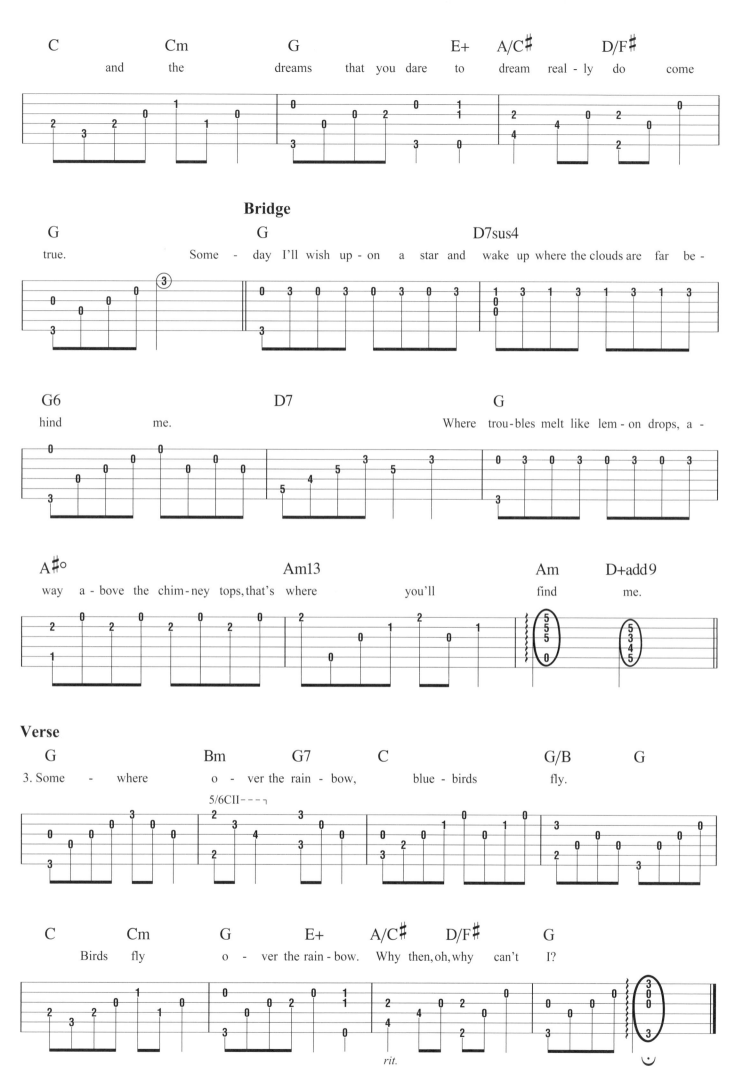

Perfect

Words and Music by Ed Sheeran

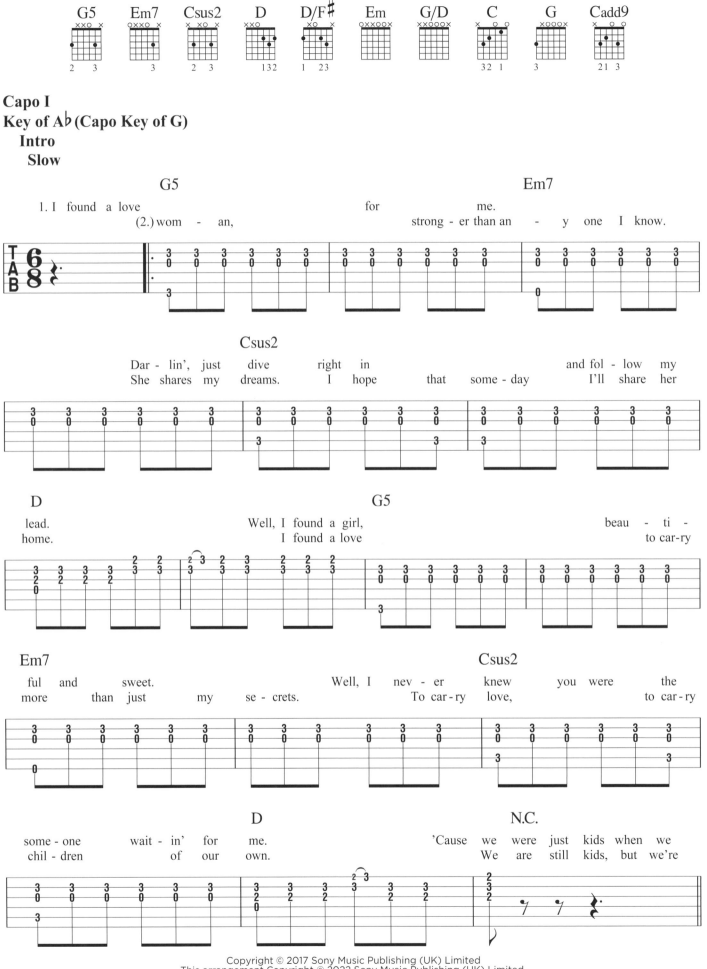

Capo I
Key of A♭ (Capo Key of G)
Intro
Slow

Pre-Chorus

G5   Em7

fell   in   love,   not know-in'   what   it   was.   I   will   not
so   in   love,   fight-in'   a - gainst   all   odds.   I   know we'll

Csus2   G5   D

give   you   up   this   time.   Dar-ling, just
be   all   right   this   time.   Dar-ling, just

G5   Em7

kiss   me   slow.   Your heart is   all   I   own.   And in your
hold   my   hand.   Be my girl, I'll   be   your   man.   I   see   my

Csus2   D   N.C.

eyes   you're   hold - ing mine. ⎫
fu - ture   hold in   your eyes. ⎬   Ba - by,

𝄋 Chorus

Em7   Csus2   G5   D

I'm   danc - in' in   the   dark   with   you   be-tween   my

Em7   Csus2   G5   D
etc.

arms,   bare - foot on   the   grass.   We're lis - ten - in' to   our

Em7   Csus2   G5   D

fav - 'rite song. ⎧ When you   said   you looked   a   mess,   I   whis-pered   un - der-neath   my
                   ⎨ When I   saw   you in   that   dress,   look - in' so   beau - ti - ful.   I
                   ⎩ I   have   faith   in what   I   see.   Now I   know   I   have met   an

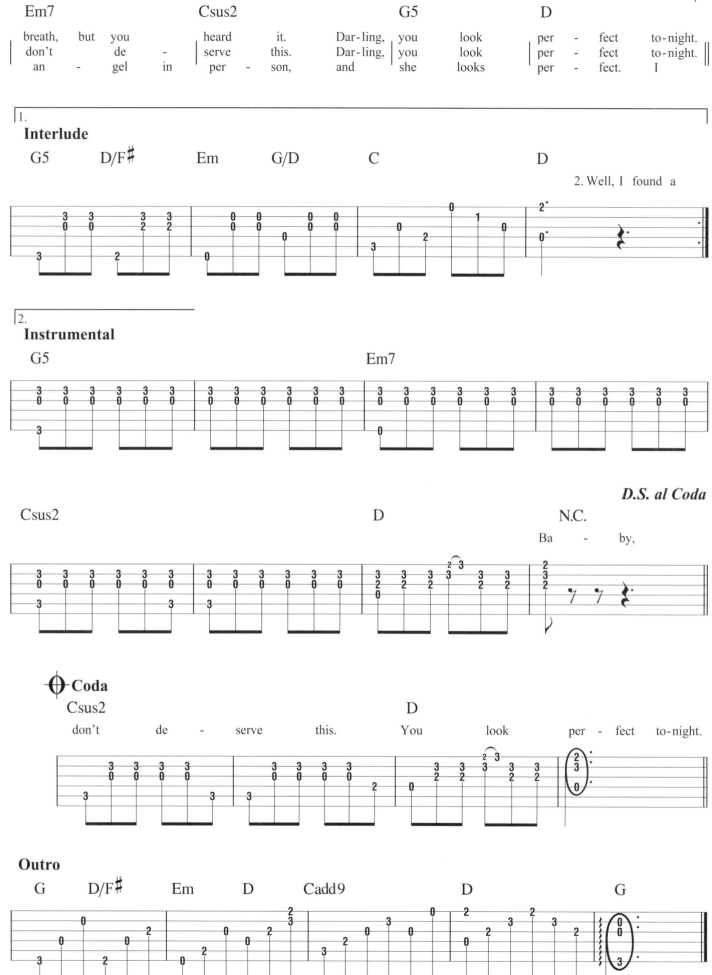

Em7	Csus2	G5	D
breath, but you	heard it.	Dar-ling, you look	per - fect to-night.
don't de -	serve this.	Dar-ling, you look	per - fect to-night.
an - gel in	per - son, and	she looks	per - fect. I

1.

Interlude

G5   D/F♯   Em   G/D   C   D

2. Well, I found a

2.

Instrumental

G5   Em7

D.S. al Coda

Csus2   D   N.C.

Ba - by,

Coda

Csus2   D

don't de - serve this.   You look   per - fect to-night.

Outro

G   D/F♯   Em   D   Cadd9   D   G

Someone Like You

Words and Music by Adele Adkins and Dan Wilson

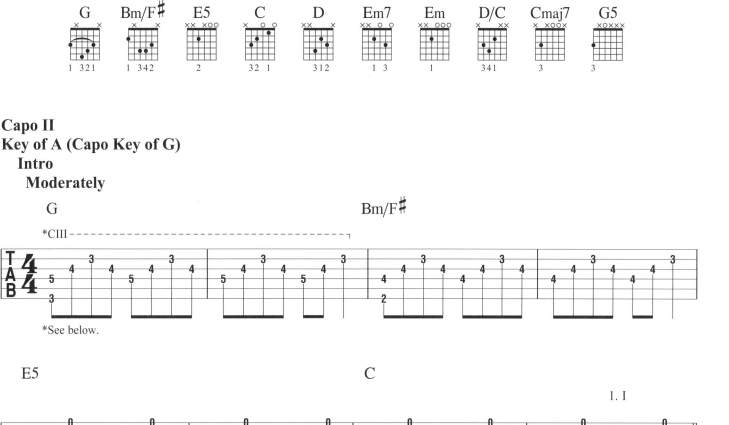

Capo II
Key of A (Capo Key of G)
  Intro
    Moderately

*See below.

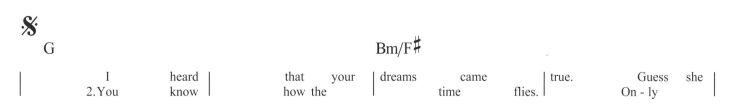

Verse
w/ Intro pattern

G   Bm/F♯

heard   that you're   set-tled down,   that you

E5   C

found a girl   and you're   mar-ried now.

𝄋
G   Bm/F♯

      I   heard   that your   dreams   came   true.   Guess she
2.You   know   how the   time   flies.   On - ly

*"C" denotes barre. Fractional prefix indicates which strings are barred (e.g. 1/2 = first 3 strings).
  Roman numeral suffix indicates barred fret.

E5   **C**

| gave you things | | I did-n't | give to you. | | Old |
| | yes-ter-day | was the | time of our lives. | | We were |

G   **Bm/F♯**

| | friend, | why are you so | shy? | Ain't like |
| born and raised | | in a | sum-mer haze | bound |

E5   **C**

| you to hold back | or | hide from the light. | | I |
| by the sur-prise | of our | glo-ry days. | | |

Pre-Chorus

D   **Em7**   **C**

hate to turn up   out of the blue   un-in-vit-ed, but I   could-n't stay a-way.

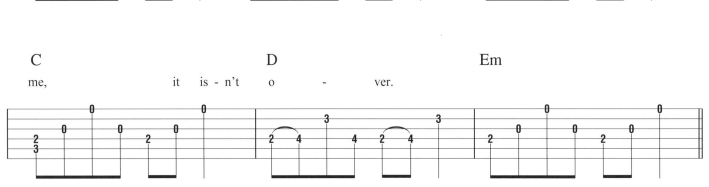

                                D   **Em7**

I could-n't fight it. I'd   hoped you'd see my face   and that you'd be re-mind-ed that for

C   **D**   **Em**

me,   it is-n't o - ver.

Chorus

G   **D**   **Em**   **C**

Nev-er-mind, I'll find   some-one like   you.   I wish

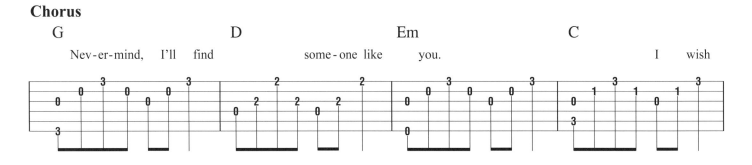

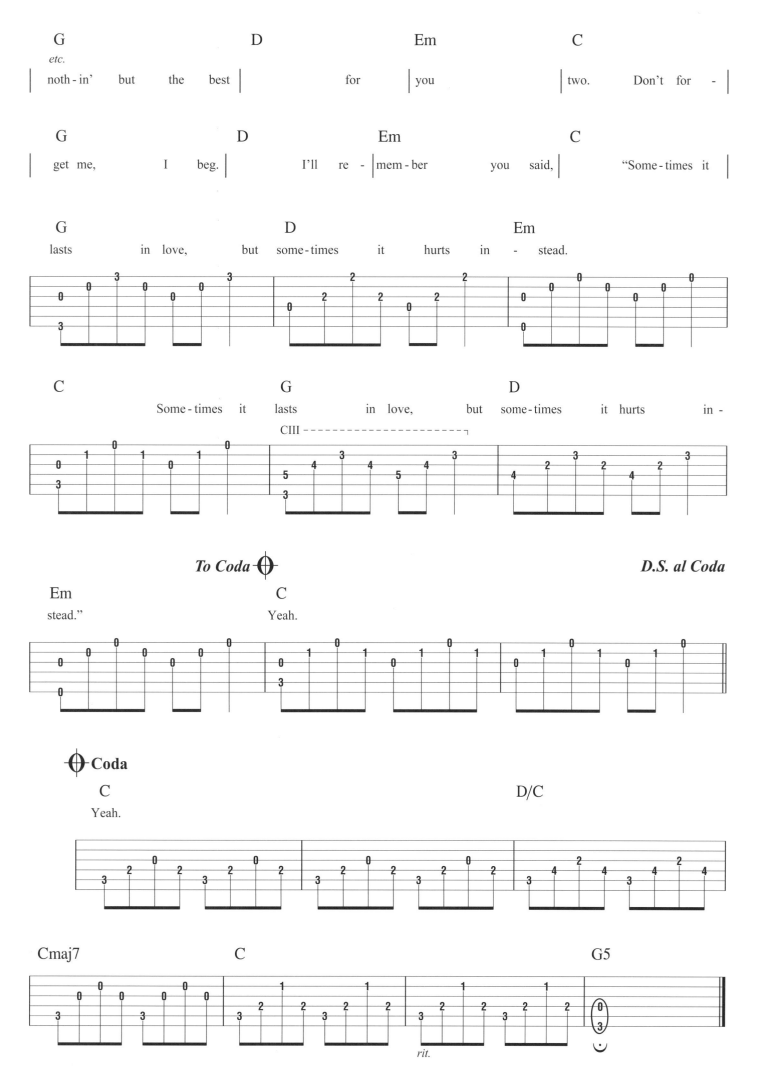

Shallow

from A STAR IS BORN

Words and Music by Stefani Germanotta, Mark Ronson, Andrew Wyatt and Anthony Rossomando

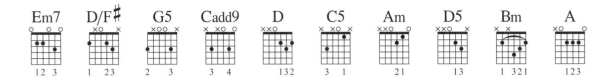

Key of G
Intro
Moderately

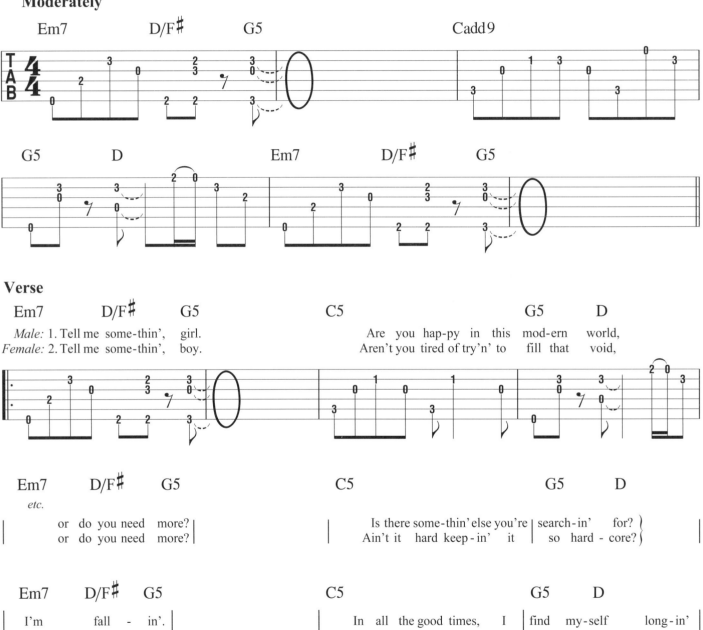

Verse

	Em7	D/F♯	G5	C5	G5	D
Male: 1.	Tell me some-thin',	girl.		Are you hap-py in this mod-ern world,		
Female: 2.	Tell me some-thin',	boy.		Aren't you tired of try'n' to fill that void,		

etc.

Em7	D/F♯	G5	C5	G5	D
or do you need more?			Is there some-thin' else you're search-in' for?		
or do you need more?			Ain't it hard keep-in' it so hard-core?		

Em7	D/F♯	G5	C5	G5	D
I'm fall-in'.			In all the good times, I find my-self long-in'		

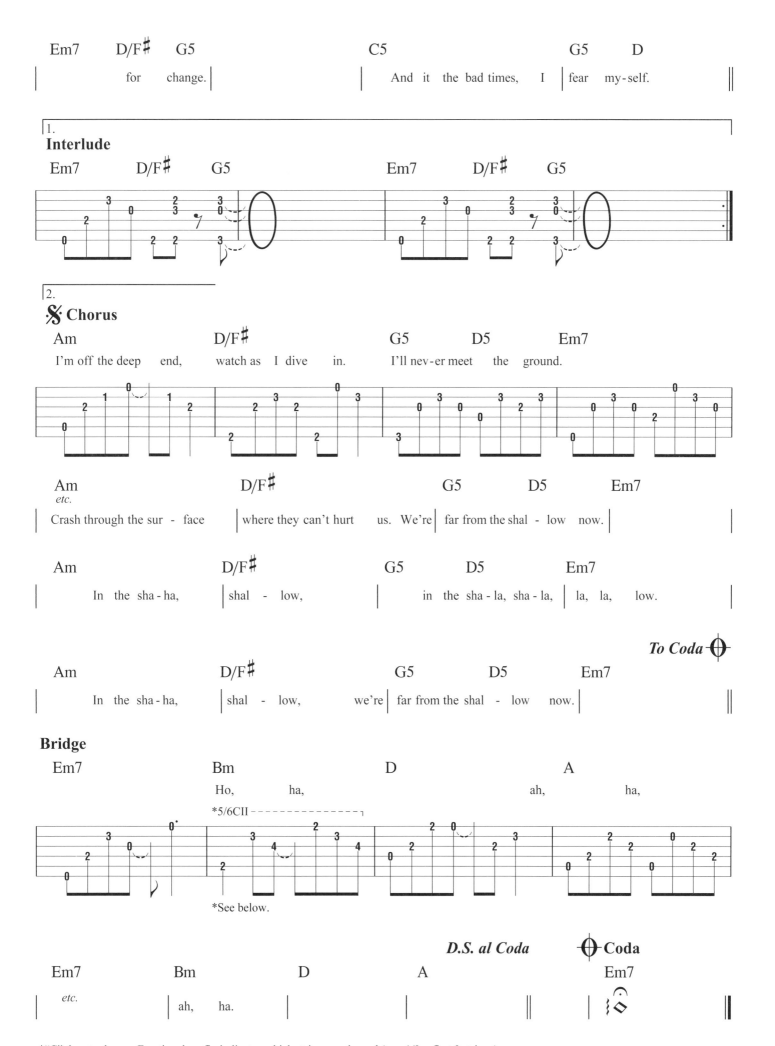

Sligo River Blues

Written by John Fahey

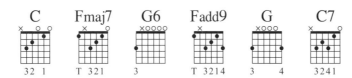

Key of C

Moderately

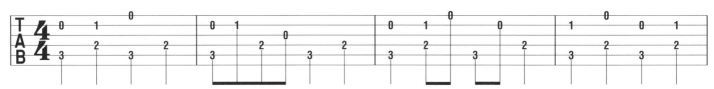

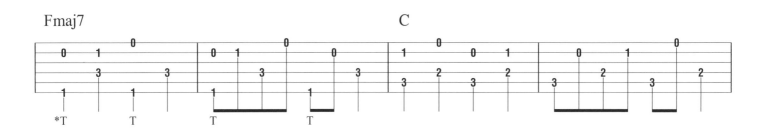

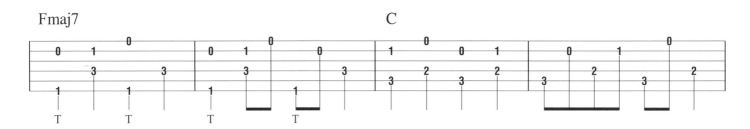

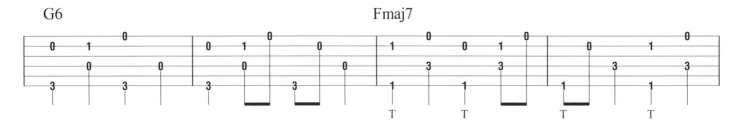

To Coda 1 ⊕

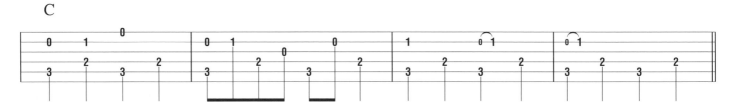

*T = Thumb on 6th string

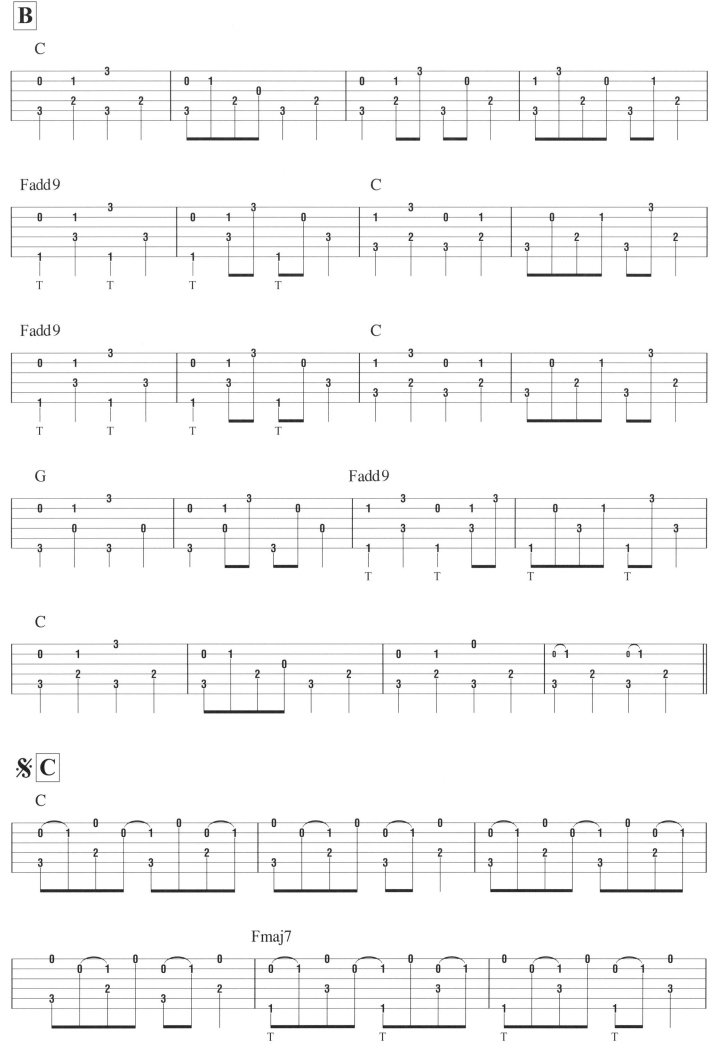

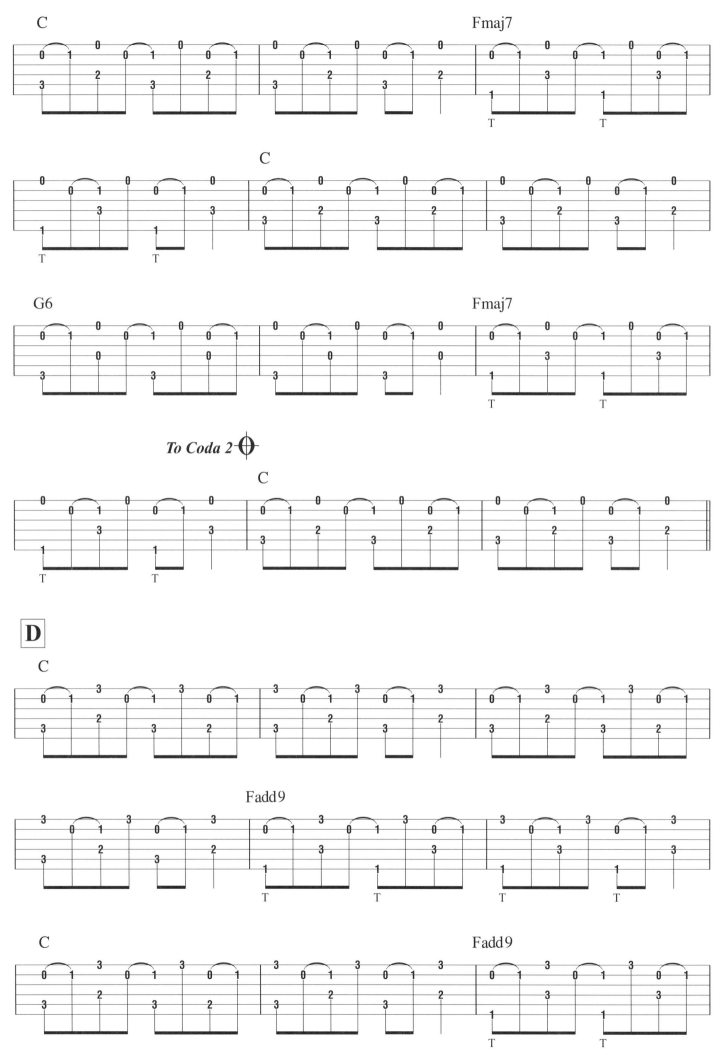

To Coda 2 ⊕

D

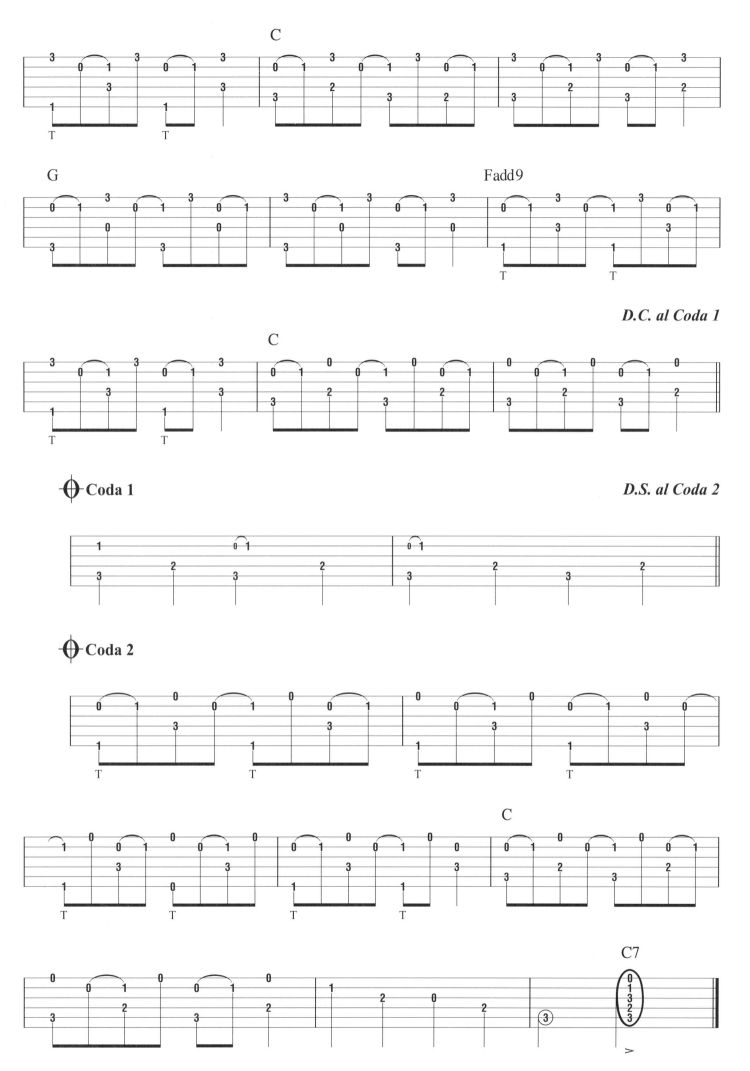

Stand By Me

featured in the Motion Picture STAND BY ME
featured in SMOKEY JOE'S CAFE

Words and Music by Jerry Leiber, Mike Stoller and Ben E. King

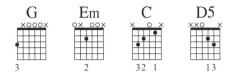

Capo II
Key of A (Capo Key of G)
　Intro
　　Moderately

1. When the night

Verse
w/ Intro pattern

G

‖: has come | | and the land is dark, |
　(2.) that we look up-| on | should tum-ble and |
3. *Instrumental*

Em

| fall, | and the moon | is the on | - ly light we'll |
| | or the moun-| tain should | crum-ble to the |

C   D

G

| see, | | no, I won't | be a-fraid, |
| sea, | | I won't cry, | I won't cry. |

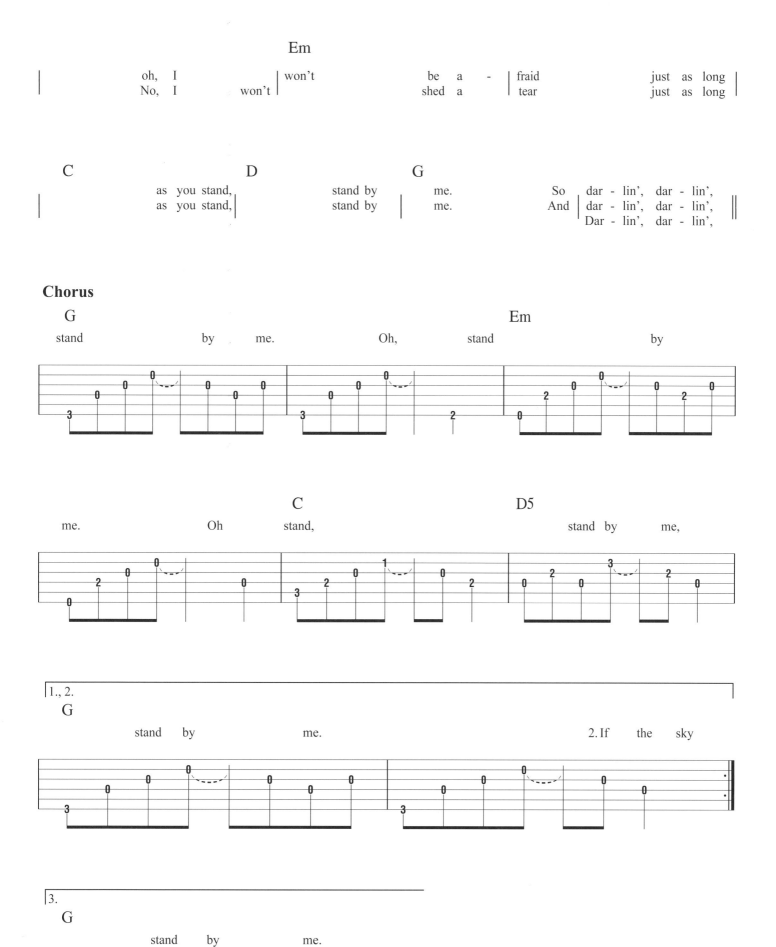

Take Me Home, Country Roads

Words and Music by John Denver, Bill Danoff and Taffy Nivert

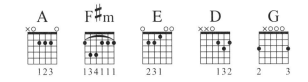

Key of A
  Intro
    Moderately fast

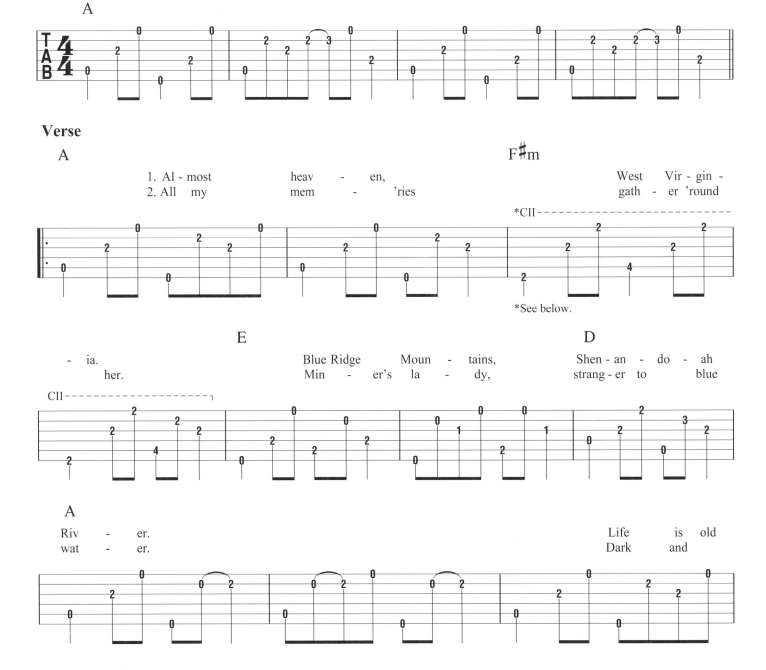

*"C" denotes barre. Fractional prefix indicates which strings are barred (e.g. 1/2 = first 3 strings).
Roman numeral suffix indicates barred fret.

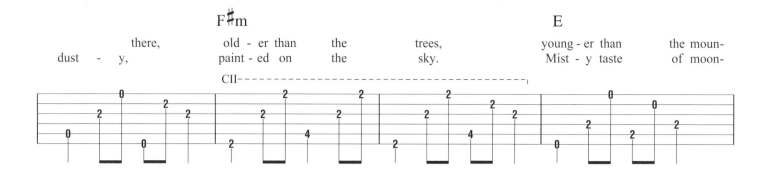

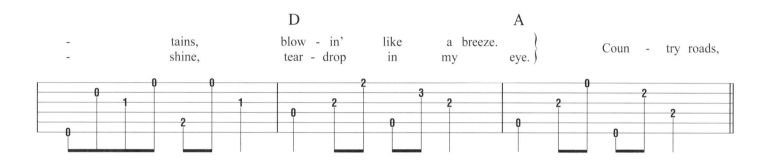

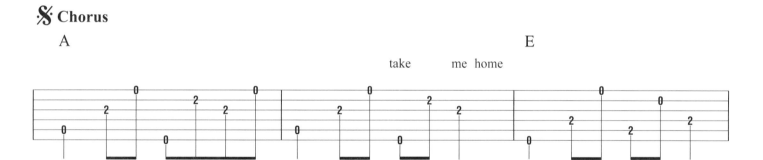

𝄉 Chorus

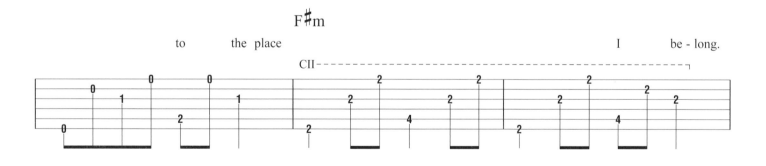

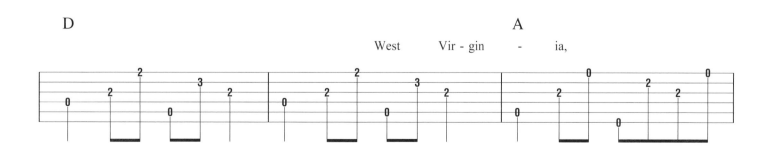

E

moun - tain ma - ma.　　　　　　　　Take　me home,

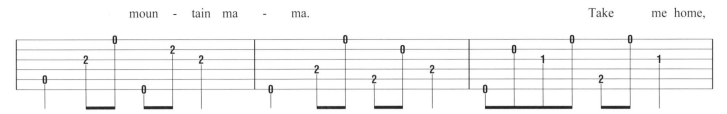

To Coda ⊕

D　　　　　　　　　　　　　　A

coun - try roads.

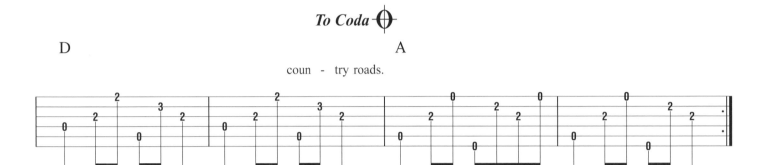

Bridge

F♯m　　　　　　　　E　　　　　　　　A

I　hear　her voice　　　in　the morn - in' hour　and she

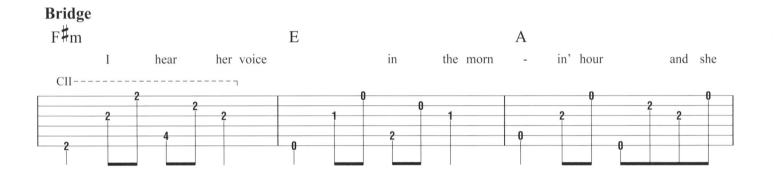

calls　me.　The　ra - di - o　re - minds　me　of　my

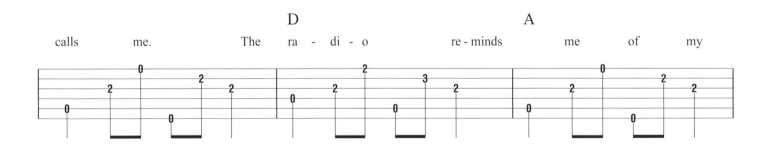

E　　　　　　　　　　　　　　　　F♯m

home　far　a - way.　　　And　driv - in' down　the road,

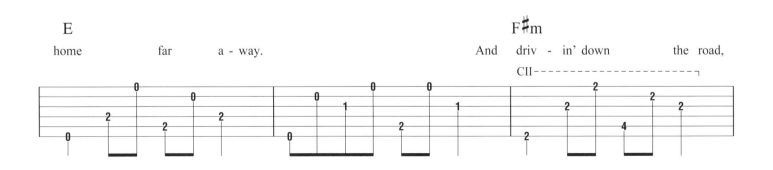

G   D   A

I   get a   feel - in'   that   I   should have been   home

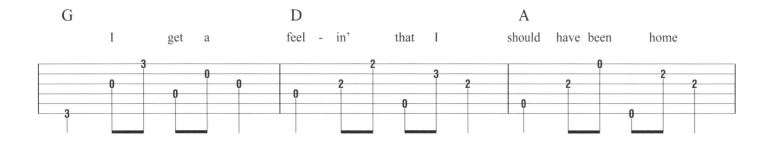

D.S. al Coda

E

yes - ter - day,   yes - ter - day.   Coun - try roads,

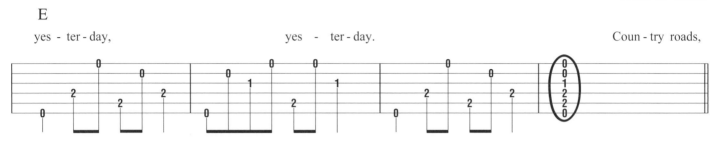

⊕ Coda

A   E

Take   me home,

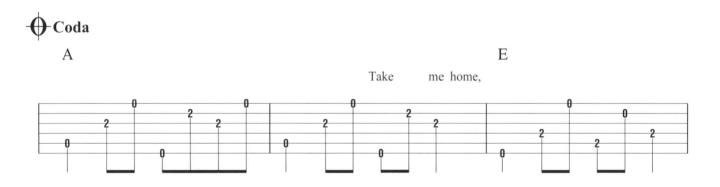

A

down   coun - try roads.   Take   me home

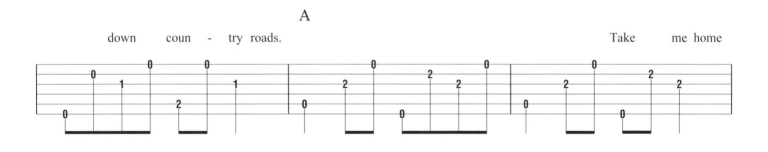

E   A

down   coun - try roads.

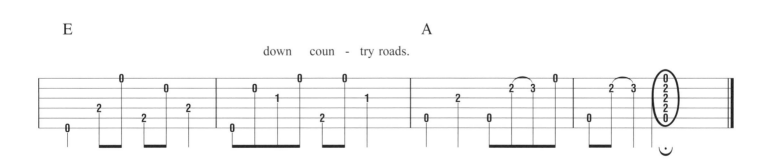

Tears in the Rain

Music by Joe Satriani

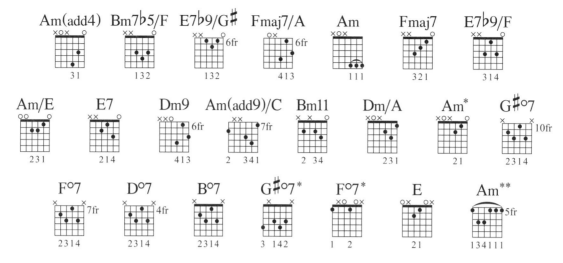

Key of Am

Moderately

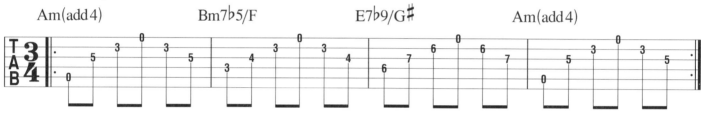

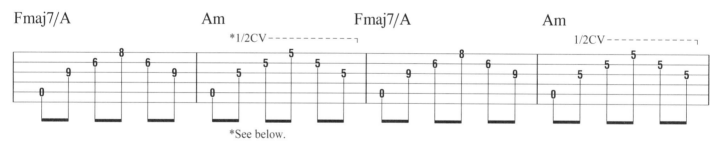

*See below.

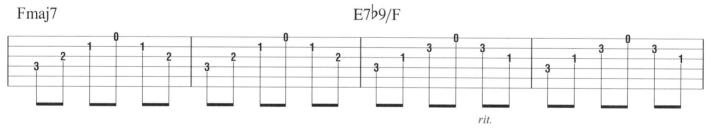

rit.

A tempo

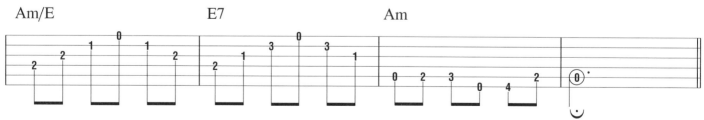

*"C" denotes barre. Fractional prefix indicates which strings are barred (e.g. 1/2 = first 3 strings).
 Roman numeral suffix indicates barred fret.

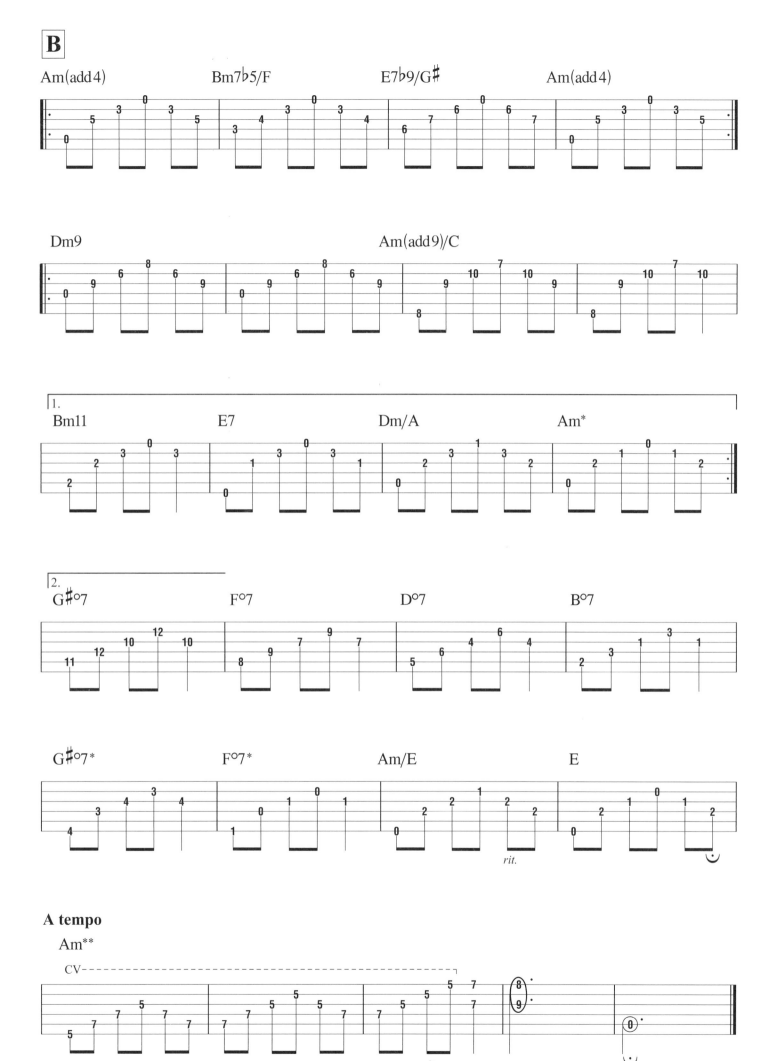

316

Words and Music by Edward Van Halen, Alex Van Halen, Michael Anthony and Sammy Hagar

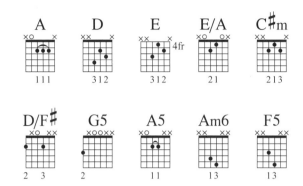

Key of A

Moderately slow

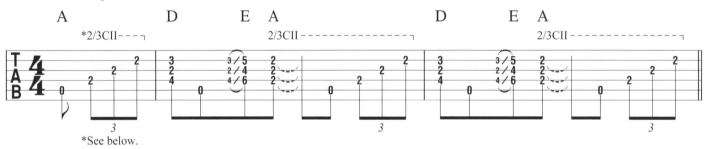

*See below.

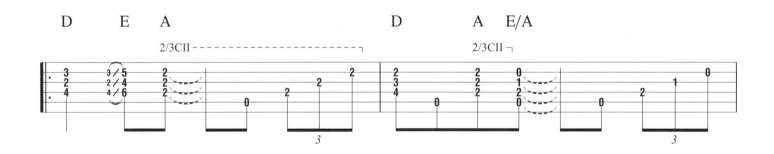

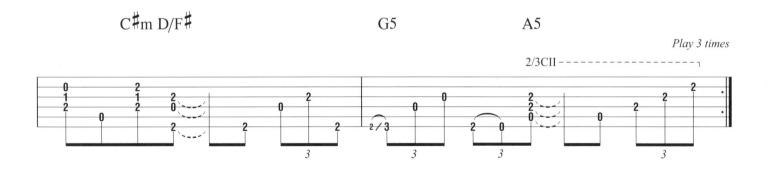

*"C" denotes barre. Fractional prefix indicates which strings are barred (e.g. 1/2 = first 3 strings).
    Roman numeral suffix indicates barred fret.

B

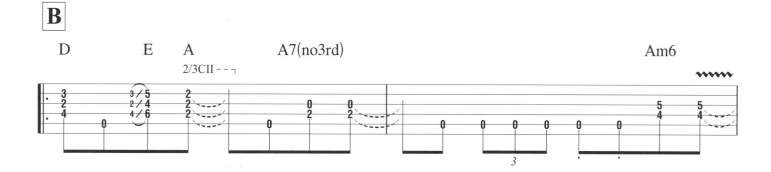

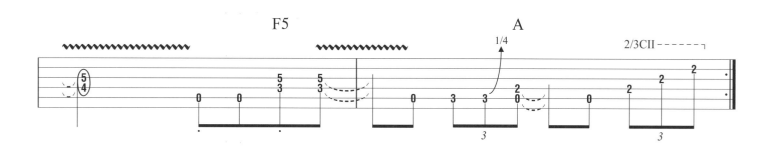

C

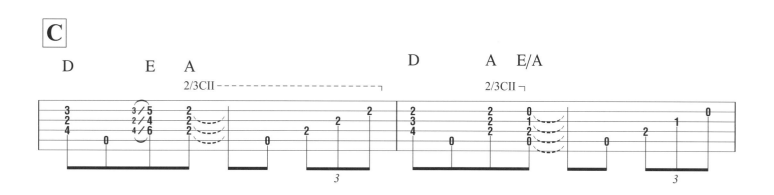

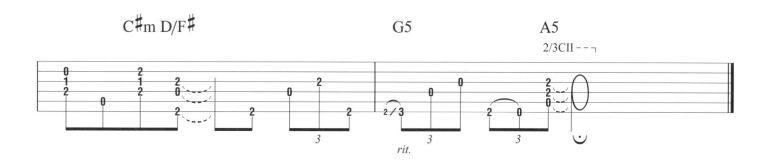

Unchained Melody

from the Motion Picture UNCHAINED

Lyric by Hy Zaret
Music by Alex North

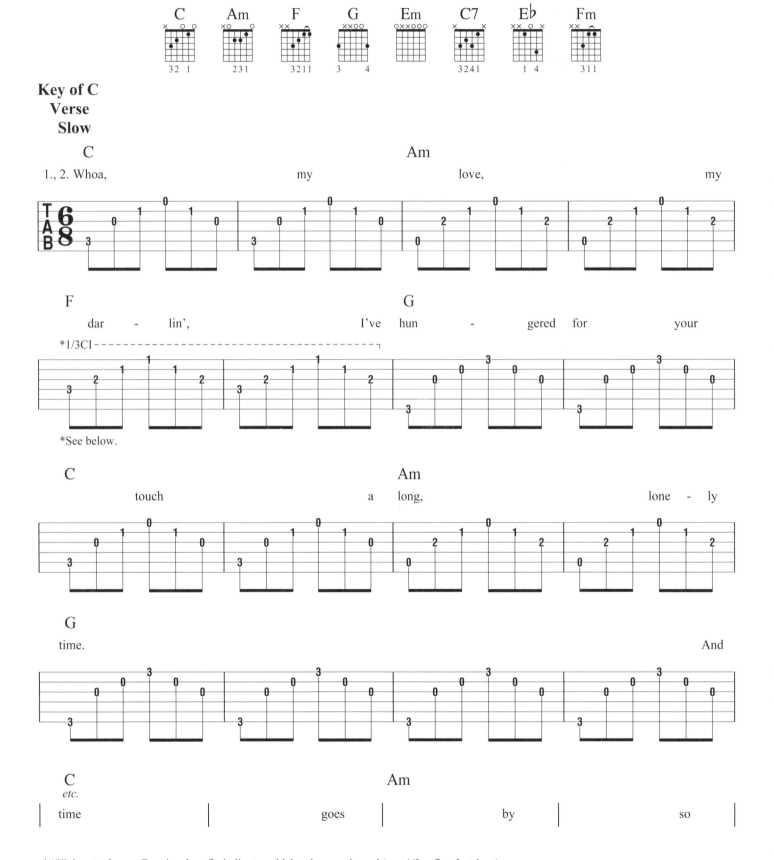

Key of C
Verse
Slow

C .... Am

1., 2. Whoa, ... my .... love, ... my

F .... G

dar - lin', ... I've hun - gered for your

*1/3CI

*See below.

C .... Am

touch .... a long, ... lone - ly

G

time. .... And

C .... Am

etc.

| time | | goes | | by | | so | |

*"C" denotes barre. Fractional prefix indicates which strings are barred (e.g. 1/2 = first 3 strings).
Roman numeral suffix indicates barred fret.

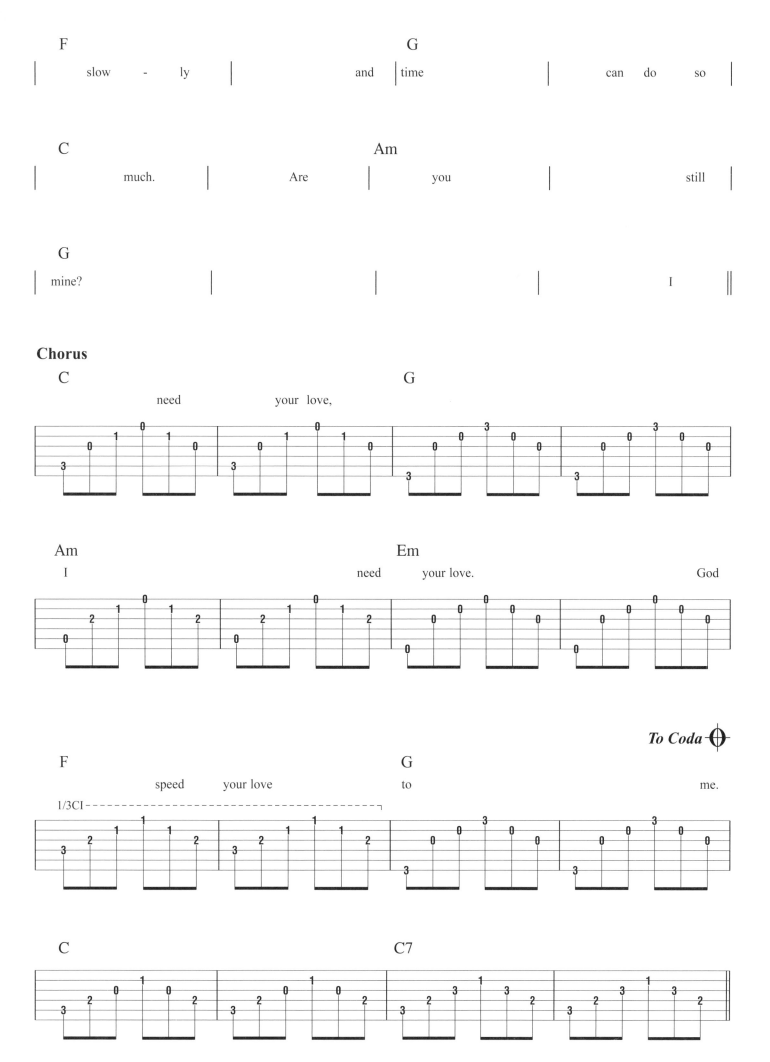

Bridge

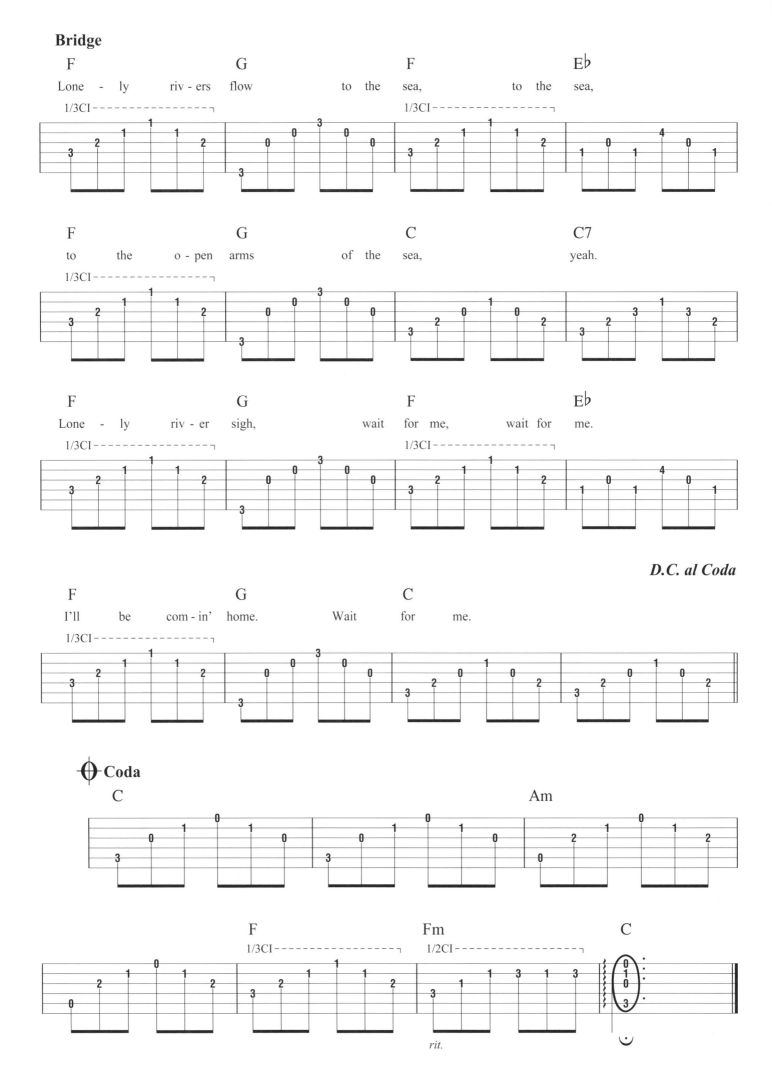

D.C. al Coda

Coda

Wonderful Tonight

Words and Music by Eric Clapton

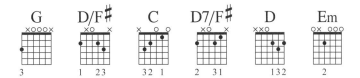

G   D/F#   C   D7/F#   D   Em

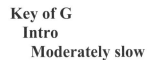

Key of G
Intro
Moderately slow

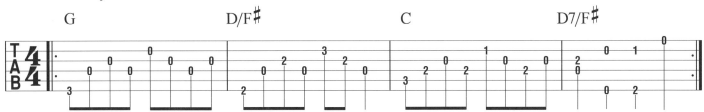

§ Verse

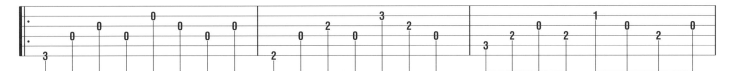

1. It's late in the eve - 'ning,   she's won - d'rin' what clothes
2. We go to a par - ty   and ev - 'ry - one turns
3. *See additional lyrics*

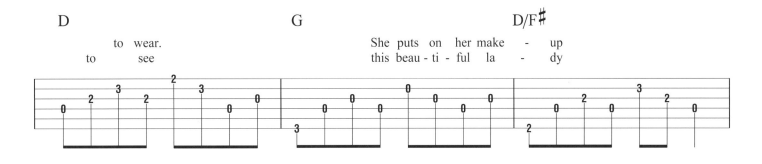

to wear.   She puts on her make - up
to see   this beau - ti - ful la - dy

and brush - es her long blonde hair.   And then she asks
that's walk - in' a - round with me.   And then she asks

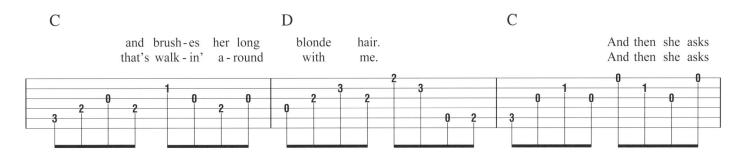

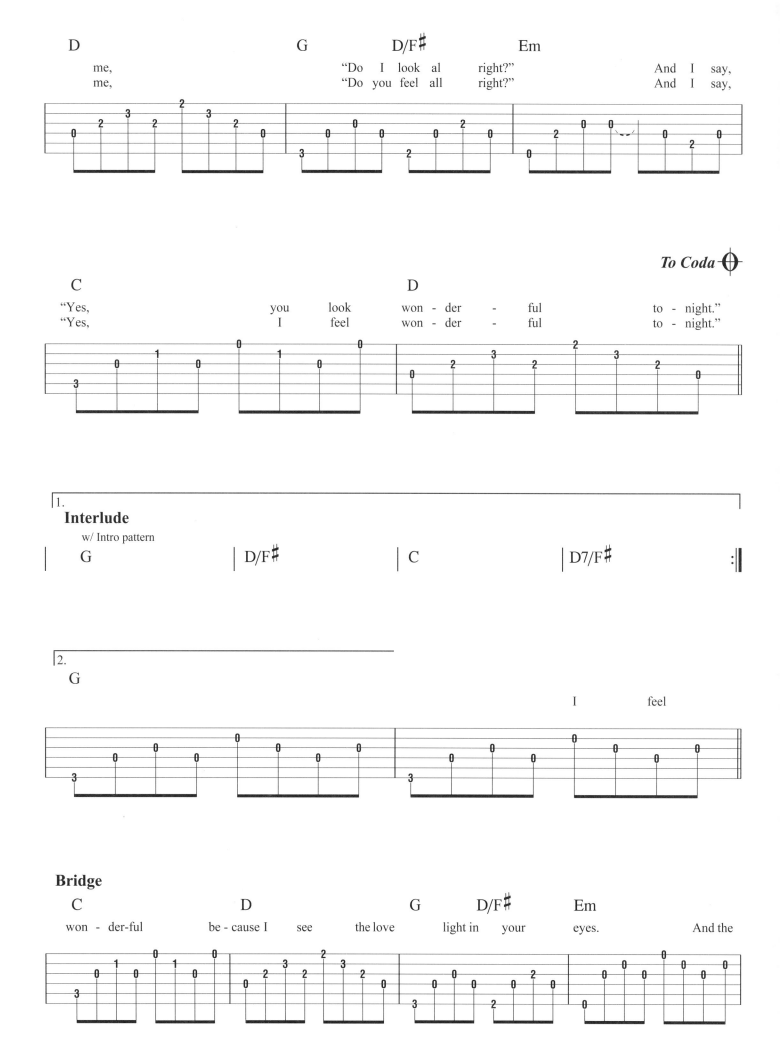

To Coda ⊕

Interlude
w/ Intro pattern

| G | D/F# | C | D7/F# |

Bridge

86

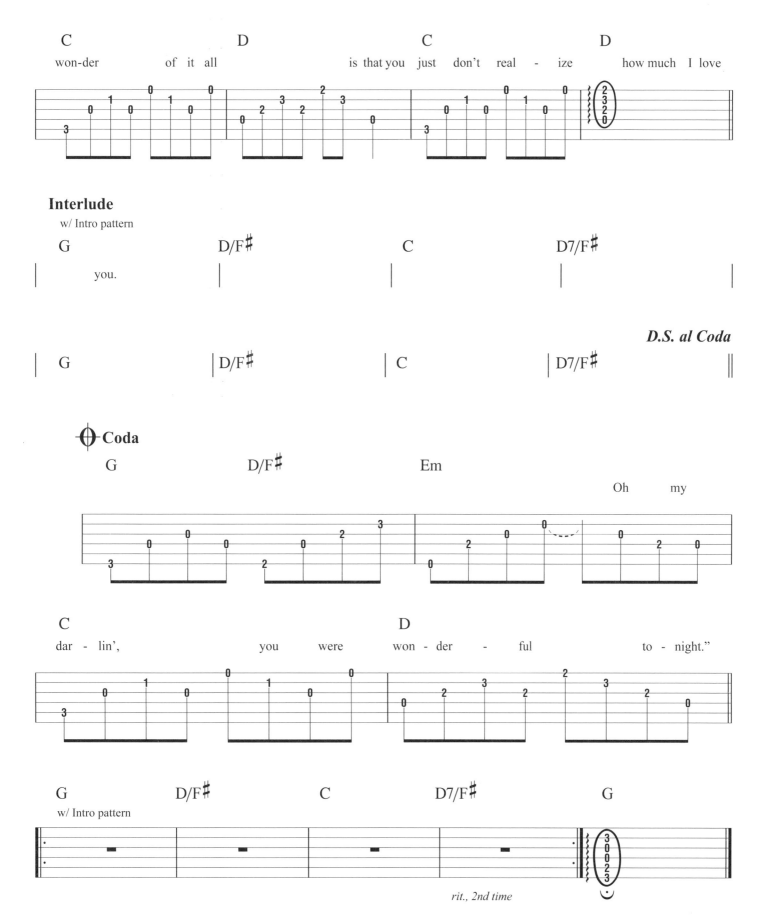

Interlude
w/ Intro pattern

D.S. al Coda

Coda

w/ Intro pattern

rit., 2nd time

Additional Lyrics

3. It's time to go home now,
   And I've got an aching head.
   So I give her the car keys
   And she helps me to bed.
   And then I tell her, as I turn out the light,
   I say, "My darlin', you were wonderful tonight.
   Oh my darlin', you were wonderful tonight."

You Are My Sunshine

Words and Music by Jimmie Davis

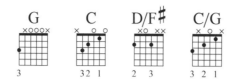

Key of G
    Intro
        Moderately fast

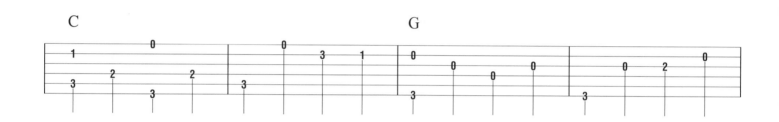

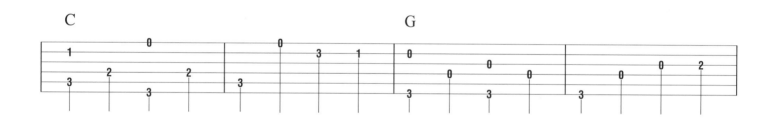

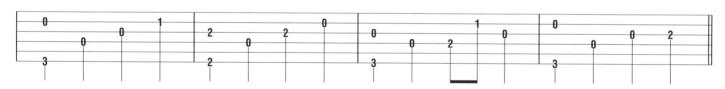

 Chorus
    w/ Intro pattern
    G

| sun - shine, | my on - ly | sun - shine. | You make me |

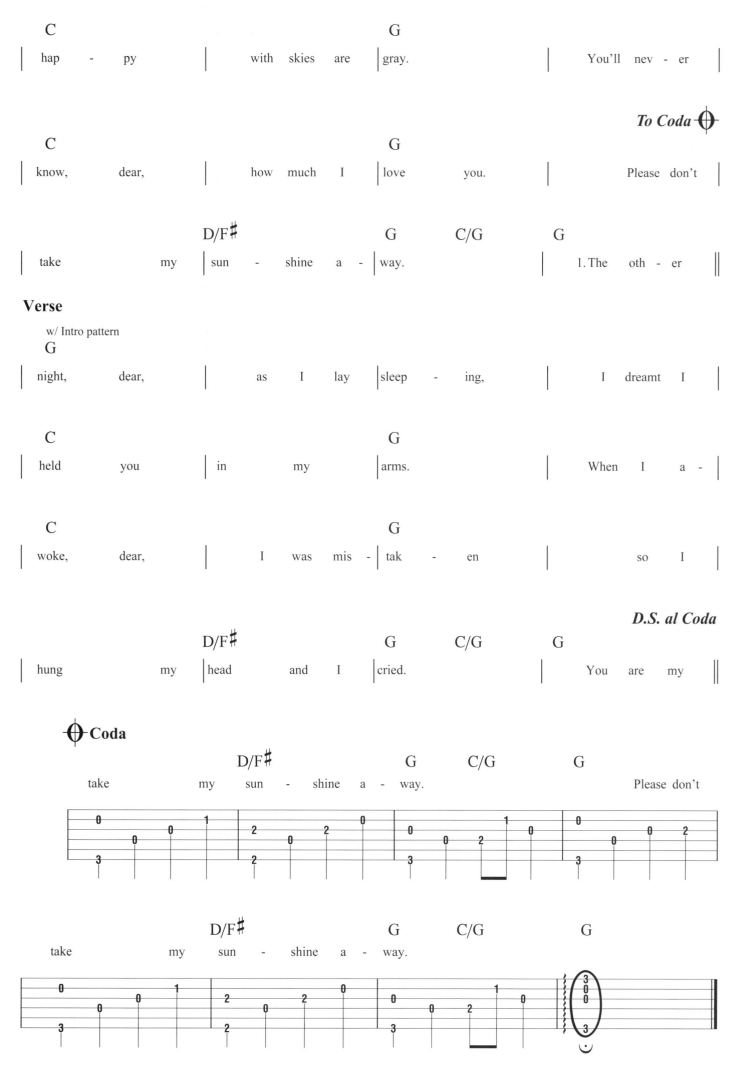

You've Got a Friend

Words and Music by Carole King

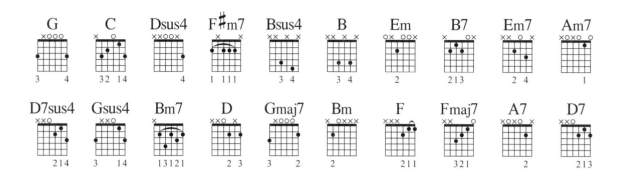

Capo II
Key of A (Capo Key of G)
  Intro
    Moderately

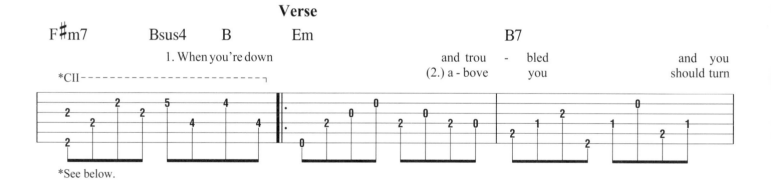

Verse

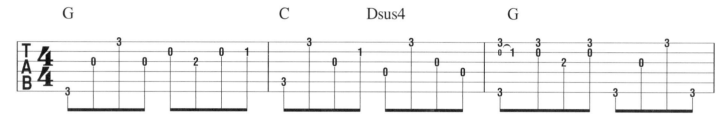

1. When you're down   and trou - bled   and you
(2.) a - bove   you   should turn

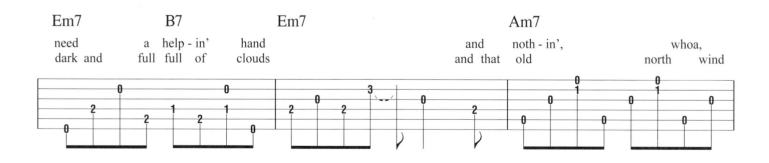

need   a help - in' hand   and noth - in',   whoa,
dark and   full full of   clouds   and that old   north wind

*"C" denotes barre. Fractional prefix indicates which strings are barred (e.g. 1/2 = first 3 strings).
  Roman numeral suffix indicates barred fret.

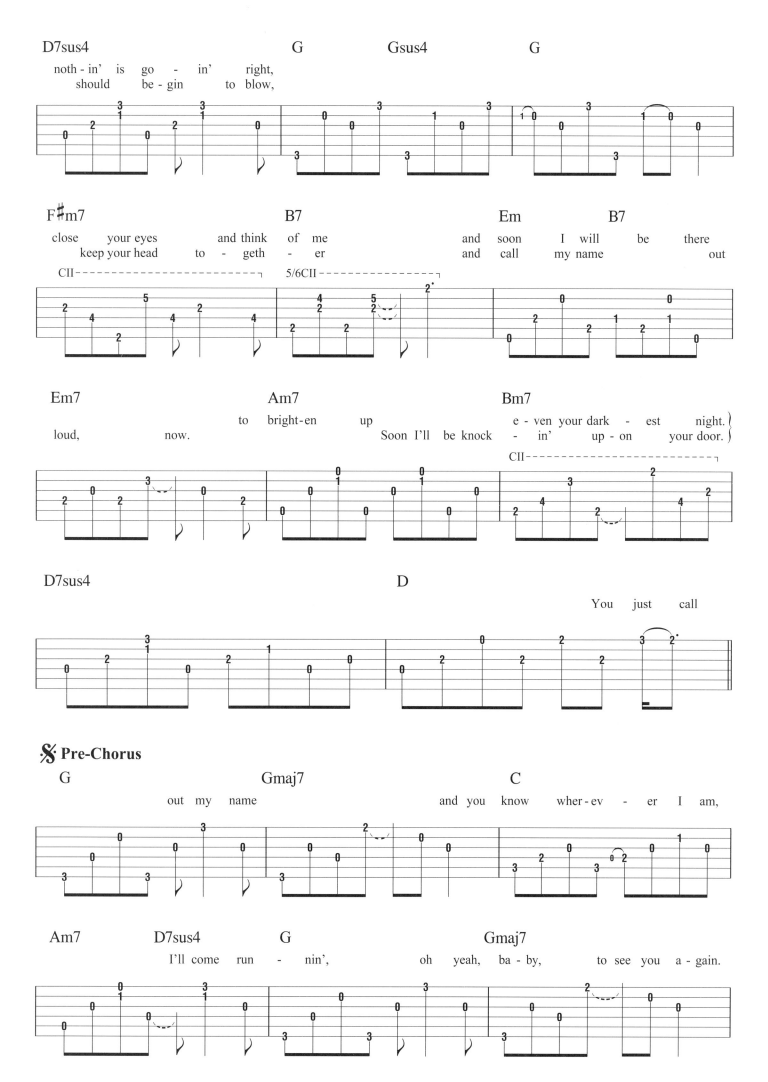

D7sus4

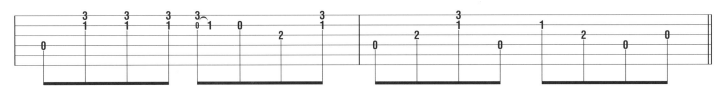

Chorus

G   Gmaj7   C

Win - ter, spring,   sum - mer of fall,   all you got to do is call

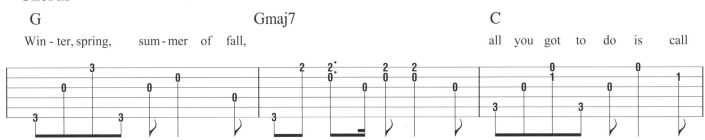

1.

To Coda ⊕

Bm   Am7   D7sus4

and I'll be there,   yeah, yeah, yeah.   You've got a friend.

Interlude

G   C   G   F♯m7   Bsus4   B

2. If the sky

CII - - - - - - - - - - - - - - -

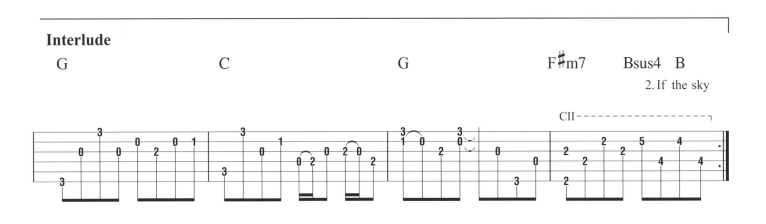

2.

Bridge

Am7   D7sus4   C   F   C

Hey, ain't   it good to know   that you've got   a friend   when

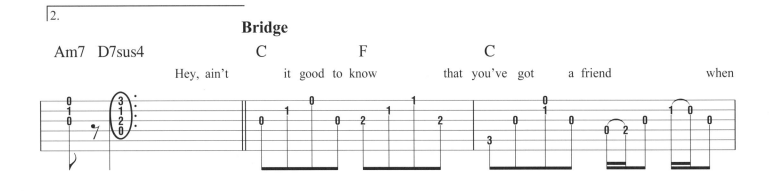

G
peo - ple can be   so   cold?

Gmaj7

C
They'll hurt you   and de - sert

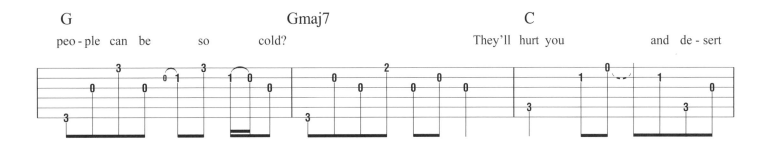

Fmaj7
you.

Em7
Well, they'll take your   soul   if   you   let

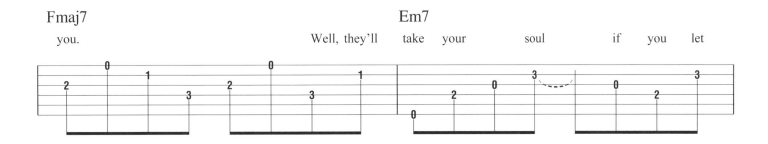

D.S. al Coda
(take 1st ending)

A7
them.   Oh,   yeah, but don't   you   let   them.

D7sus4

D7
You just   call

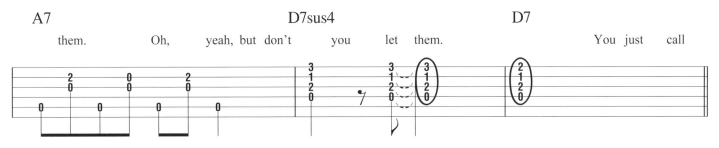

Coda

G   C

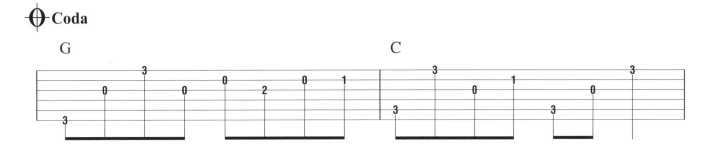

G   C   G
You've got   a friend.

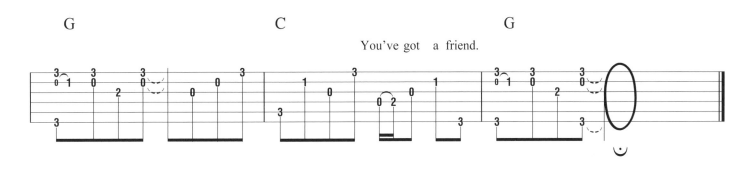

Get Better at Guitar

...with these Great Guitar Instruction Books from Hal Leonard!

101 GUITAR TIPS
INCLUDES TAB

STUFF ALL THE PROS KNOW AND USE

by Adam St. James

This book contains invaluable guidance on everything from scales and music theory to truss rod adjustments, proper recording studio set-ups, and much more.

00695737 Book/Online Audio $17.99

AMAZING PHRASING
INCLUDES TAB

by Tom Kolb

This book/audio pack explores all the main components necessary for crafting well-balanced rhythmic and melodic phrases. It also explains how these phrases are put together to form cohesive solos. The companion audio contains 89 demo tracks, most with full-band backing.

00695583 Book/Online Audio $22.99

ARPEGGIOS FOR THE MODERN GUITARIST
INCLUDES TAB

by Tom Kolb

Using this no-nonsense book with online audio, guitarists will learn to apply and execute all types of arpeggio forms using a variety of techniques, including alternate picking, sweep picking, tapping, string skipping, and legato.

00695862 Book/Online Audio $22.99

BLUES YOU CAN USE

by John Ganapes

This comprehensive source for learning blues guitar is designed to develop both your lead and rhythm playing. Includes: 21 complete solos • blues chords, progressions and riffs • turnarounds • movable scales and soloing techniques • string bending • utilizing the entire fingerboard • and more.

00142420 Book/Online Media..................................$22.99

CONNECTING PENTATONIC PATTERNS
INCLUDES TAB

by Tom Kolb

If you've been finding yourself trapped in the pentatonic box, this book is for you! This hands-on book with online audio offers examples for guitar players of all levels, from beginner to advanced. Study this book faithfully, and soon you'll be soloing all over the neck with the greatest of ease.

00696445 Book/Online Audio $24.99

FRETBOARD MASTERY
INCLUDES TAB

by Troy Stetina

Untangle the mysterious regions of the guitar fretboard and unlock your potential. This book familiarizes you with all the shapes you need to know by applying them in real musical examples, thereby reinforcing and reaffirming your newfound knowledge.

00695331 Book/Online Audio $22.99

GUITAR AEROBICS
INCLUDES TAB

by Troy Nelson

Here is a daily dose of guitar "vitamins" to keep your chops fine tuned! Musical styles include rock, blues, jazz, metal, country, and funk. Techniques taught include alternate picking, arpeggios, sweep picking, string skipping, legato, string bending, and rhythm guitar.

00695946 Book/Online Audio $24.99

GUITAR CLUES
INCLUDES TAB

OPERATION PENTATONIC

by Greg Koch

Whether you're new to improvising or have been doing it for a while, this book/audio pack will provide loads of delicious licks and tricks that you can use right away, from volume swells and chicken pickin' to intervallic and chordal ideas.

00695827 Book/Online Audio $19.99

PAT METHENY – GUITAR ETUDES
INCLUDES TAB

Over the years, in many master classes and workshops around the world, Pat has demonstrated the kind of daily workout he puts himself through. This book includes a collection of 14 guitar etudes he created to help you limber up, improve picking technique and build finger independence.

00696587..$17.99

PICTURE CHORD ENCYCLOPEDIA

This comprehensive guitar chord resource for all playing styles and levels features five voicings of 44 chord qualities for all twelve keys – 2,640 chords in all! For each, there is a clearly illustrated chord frame, as well as *an actual photo* of the chord being played!.

00695224..$22.99

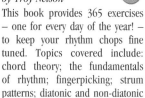

RHYTHM GUITAR 365
INCLUDES TAB

by Troy Nelson

This book provides 365 exercises – one for every day of the year! – to keep your rhythm chops fine tuned. Topics covered include: chord theory; the fundamentals of rhythm; fingerpicking; strum patterns; diatonic and non-diatonic progressions; triads; major and minor keys; and more.

00103627 Book/Online Audio $27.99

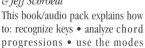

SCALE CHORD RELATIONSHIPS
INCLUDES TAB

by Michael Mueller & Jeff Schroedl

This book/audio pack explains how to: recognize keys • analyze chord progressions • use the modes • play over nondiatonic harmony • use harmonic and melodic minor scales • use symmetrical scales • incorporate exotic scales • and much more!

00695563 Book/Online Audio $17.99

SPEED MECHANICS FOR LEAD GUITAR
INCLUDES TAB

by Troy Stetina

Take your playing to the stratosphere with this advanced lead book which will help you develop speed and precision in today's explosive playing styles. Learn the fastest ways to achieve speed and control, secrets to make your practice time really count, and how to open your ears and make your musical ideas more solid and tangible.

00699323 Book/Online Audio $22.99

TOTAL ROCK GUITAR
INCLUDES TAB

by Troy Stetina

This comprehensive source for learning rock guitar is designed to develop both lead and rhythm playing. It covers: getting a tone that rocks • open chords, power chords and barre chords • riffs, scales and licks • string bending, strumming, and harmonics • and more.

00695246 Book/Online Audio $22.99

Guitar World Presents
STEVE VAI'S GUITAR WORKOUT
INCLUDES TAB

In this book, Steve Vai reveals his path to virtuoso enlightenment with two challenging guitar workouts – one 10-hour and one 30-hour – which include scale and chord exercises, ear training, sight-reading, music theory, and much more.

00119643..$16.99

HAL•LEONARD®

FINGERPICKING GUITAR BOOKS

Hone your fingerpicking skills with these great songbooks featuring solo guitar arrangements in standard notation and tablature. The arrangements in these books are carefully written for intermediate-level guitarists. Each song combines melody and harmony in one superb guitar fingerpicking arrangement. Each book also includes an introduction to basic fingerstyle guitar.

 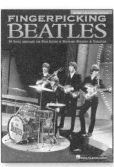    

Fingerpicking Acoustic
00699614 15 songs........................$14.99

Fingerpicking Acoustic Classics
00160211 15 songs........................$16.99

Fingerpicking Acoustic Hits
00160202 15 songs........................$12.99

Fingerpicking Acoustic Rock
00699764 14 songs........................$16.99

Fingerpicking Ballads
00699717 15 songs........................$14.99

Fingerpicking Beatles
00699049 30 songs........................$24.99

Fingerpicking Beethoven
00702390 15 pieces.......................$10.99

Fingerpicking Blues
00701277 15 songs........................$10.99

Fingerpicking Broadway Favorites
00699843 15 songs........................$9.99

Fingerpicking Broadway Hits
00699838 15 songs........................$7.99

Fingerpicking Campfire
00275964 15 songs........................$12.99

Fingerpicking Celtic Folk
00701148 15 songs........................$12.99

Fingerpicking Children's Songs
00699712 15 songs........................$9.99

Fingerpicking Christian
00701076 15 songs........................$12.99

Fingerpicking Christmas
00699599 20 carols.......................$10.99

Fingerpicking Christmas Classics
00701695 15 songs........................$7.99

Fingerpicking Christmas Songs
00171333 15 songs........................$10.99

Fingerpicking Classical
00699620 15 pieces.......................$10.99

Fingerpicking Country
00699687 17 songs........................$12.99

Fingerpicking Disney
00699711 15 songs........................$16.99

Fingerpicking Early Jazz Standards
00276565 15 songs........................$12.99

Fingerpicking Duke Ellington
00699845 15 songs........................$9.99

Fingerpicking Enya
00701161 15 songs........................$16.99

Fingerpicking Film Score Music
00160143 15 songs........................$12.99

Fingerpicking Gospel
00701059 15 songs........................$9.99

Fingerpicking Hit Songs
00160195 15 songs........................$12.99

Fingerpicking Hymns
00699688 15 hymns.......................$12.99

Fingerpicking Irish Songs
00701965 15 songs........................$10.99

Fingerpicking Italian Songs
00159778 15 songs........................$12.99

Fingerpicking Jazz Favorites
00699844 15 songs........................$12.99

Fingerpicking Jazz Standards
00699840 15 songs........................$12.99

Fingerpicking Elton John
00237495 15 songs........................$14.99

Fingerpicking Latin Favorites
00699842 15 songs........................$12.99

Fingerpicking Latin Standards
00699837 15 songs........................$17.99

Fingerpicking Andrew Lloyd Webber
00699839 14 songs........................$16.99

Fingerpicking Love Songs
00699841 15 songs........................$14.99

Fingerpicking Love Standards
00699836 15 songs........................$9.99

Fingerpicking Lullabyes
00701276 16 songs........................$9.99

Fingerpicking Movie Music
00699919 15 songs........................$14.99

Fingerpicking Mozart
00699794 15 pieces.......................$10.99

Fingerpicking Pop
00699615 15 songs........................$14.99

Fingerpicking Popular Hits
00139079 14 songs........................$12.99

Fingerpicking Praise
00699714 15 songs........................$14.99

Fingerpicking Rock
00699716 15 songs........................$14.99

Fingerpicking Standards
00699613 17 songs........................$14.99

Fingerpicking Wedding
00699637 15 songs........................$10.99

Fingerpicking Worship
00700554 15 songs........................$14.99

Fingerpicking Neil Young – Greatest Hits
00700134 16 songs........................$16.99

Fingerpicking Yuletide
00699654 16 songs........................$12.99

HAL•LEONARD®

Order these and more great publications from your favorite music retailer at
halleonard.com

Prices, contents and availability subject to change without notice.

0322
279

    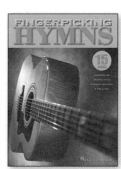 

EASY GUITAR WITH NOTES & TAB

This series features simplified arrangements with notes, tab, chord charts, and strum and pick patterns.

MIXED FOLIOS

00702287	Acoustic	$19.99
00702002	Acoustic Rock Hits for Easy Guitar	$15.99
00702166	All-Time Best Guitar Collection	$19.99
00702232	Best Acoustic Songs for Easy Guitar	$16.99
00119835	Best Children's Songs	$16.99
00703055	The Big Book of Nursery Rhymes & Children's Songs	$16.99
00698978	Big Christmas Collection	$19.99
00702394	Bluegrass Songs for Easy Guitar	$15.99
00289632	Bohemian Rhapsody	$19.99
00703387	Celtic Classics	$14.99
00224808	Chart Hits of 2016-2017	$14.99
00267383	Chart Hits of 2017-2018	$14.99
00334293	Chart Hits of 2019-2020	$16.99
00702149	Children's Christian Songbook	$9.99
00702028	Christmas Classics	$8.99
00101779	Christmas Guitar	$14.99
00702141	Classic Rock	$8.95
00159642	Classical Melodies	$12.99
00253933	Disney/Pixar's Coco	$16.99
00702203	CMT's 100 Greatest Country Songs	$34.99
00702283	The Contemporary Christian Collection	$16.99
00196954	Contemporary Disney	$19.99
00702239	Country Classics for Easy Guitar	$24.99

00702257	Easy Acoustic Guitar Songs	$16.99
00702041	Favorite Hymns for Easy Guitar	$12.99
00222701	Folk Pop Songs	$17.99
00126894	Frozen	$14.99
00333922	Frozen 2	$14.99
00702286	Glee	$16.99
00702160	The Great American Country Songbook	$19.99
00702148	Great American Gospel for Guitar	$14.99
00702050	Great Classical Themes for Easy Guitar	$9.99
00275088	The Greatest Showman	$17.99
00148030	Halloween Guitar Songs	$14.99
00702273	Irish Songs	$12.99
00192503	Jazz Classics for Easy Guitar	$16.99
00702275	Jazz Favorites for Easy Guitar	$17.99
00702274	Jazz Standards for Easy Guitar	$19.99
00702162	Jumbo Easy Guitar Songbook	$24.99
00232285	La La Land	$16.99
00702258	Legends of Rock	$14.99
00702189	MTV's 100 Greatest Pop Songs	$34.99
00702272	1950s Rock	$16.99
00702271	1960s Rock	$16.99
00702270	1970s Rock	$19.99
00702269	1980s Rock	$15.99
00702268	1990s Rock	$19.99
00369043	Rock Songs for Kids	$14.99

00109725	Once	$14.99
00702187	Selections from O Brother Where Art Thou?	$19.99
00702178	100 Songs for Kids	$14.99
00702515	Pirates of the Caribbean	$17.99
00702125	Praise and Worship for Guitar	$14.99
00287930	Songs from A Star Is Born, The Greatest Showman, La La Land, and More Movie Musicals	$16.99
00702285	Southern Rock Hits	$12.99
00156420	Star Wars Music	$16.99
00121535	30 Easy Celtic Guitar Solos	$16.99
00702156	3-Chord Rock	$12.99
00244654	Top Hits of 2017	$14.99
00283786	Top Hits of 2018	$14.99
00702294	Top Worship Hits	$17.99
00702255	VH1's 100 Greatest Hard Rock Songs	$34.99
00702175	VH1's 100 Greatest Songs of Rock and Roll	$29.99
00702253	Wicked	$12.99

ARTIST COLLECTIONS

00702267	AC/DC for Easy Guitar	$16.99
00702598	Adele for Easy Guitar	$15.99
00156221	Adele – 25	$16.99
00702040	Best of the Allman Brothers	$16.99
00702865	J.S. Bach for Easy Guitar	$15.99
00702169	Best of The Beach Boys	$15.99
00702292	The Beatles — 1	$22.99
00125796	Best of Chuck Berry	$15.99
00702201	The Essential Black Sabbath	$15.99
00702250	blink-182 — Greatest Hits	$17.99
02501615	Zac Brown Band — The Foundation	$17.99
02501621	Zac Brown Band — You Get What You Give	$16.99
00702043	Best of Johnny Cash	$17.99
00702090	Eric Clapton's Best	$16.99
00702086	Eric Clapton — from the Album Unplugged	$17.99
00702202	The Essential Eric Clapton	$17.99
00702053	Best of Patsy Cline	$15.99
00222697	Very Best of Coldplay – 2nd Edition	$16.99
00702229	The Very Best of Creedence Clearwater Revival	$16.99
00702145	Best of Jim Croce	$16.99
00702278	Crosby, Stills & Nash	$12.99
14042809	Bob Dylan	$15.99
00702276	Fleetwood Mac — Easy Guitar Collection	$17.99
00139462	The Very Best of Grateful Dead	$16.99
00702136	Best of Merle Haggard	$16.99
00702227	Jimi Hendrix — Smash Hits	$19.99
00702288	Best of Hillsong United	$12.99
00702236	Best of Antonio Carlos Jobim	$15.99
00702245	Elton John — Greatest Hits 1970–2002	$19.99

00129855	Jack Johnson	$16.99
00702204	Robert Johnson	$14.99
00702234	Selections from Toby Keith — 35 Biggest Hits	$12.95
00702003	Kiss	$16.99
00702216	Lynyrd Skynyrd	$16.99
00702182	The Essential Bob Marley	$16.99
00146081	Maroon 5	$14.99
00121925	Bruno Mars — Unorthodox Jukebox	$12.99
00702248	Paul McCartney — All the Best	$14.99
00125484	The Best of MercyMe	$12.99
00702209	Steve Miller Band — Young Hearts (Greatest Hits)	$12.95
00124167	Jason Mraz	$15.99
00702096	Best of Nirvana	$16.99
00702211	The Offspring — Greatest Hits	$17.99
00138026	One Direction	$17.99
00702030	Best of Roy Orbison	$17.99
00702144	Best of Ozzy Osbourne	$14.99
00702279	Tom Petty	$17.99
00102911	Pink Floyd	$17.99
00702139	Elvis Country Favorites	$19.99
00702293	The Very Best of Prince	$19.99
00699415	Best of Queen for Guitar	$16.99
00109279	Best of R.E.M.	$14.99
00702208	Red Hot Chili Peppers — Greatest Hits	$16.99
00198960	The Rolling Stones	$17.99
00174793	The Very Best of Santana	$16.99
00702196	Best of Bob Seger	$16.99
00146046	Ed Sheeran	$15.99
00702252	Frank Sinatra — Nothing But the Best	$12.99
00702010	Best of Rod Stewart	$17.99
00702049	Best of George Strait	$17.99

00702259	Taylor Swift for Easy Guitar	$15.99
00359800	Taylor Swift – Easy Guitar Anthology	$24.99
00702260	Taylor Swift — Fearless	$14.99
00139727	Taylor Swift — 1989	$17.99
00115960	Taylor Swift — Red	$16.99
00253667	Taylor Swift — Reputation	$17.99
00702290	Taylor Swift — Speak Now	$16.99
00232849	Chris Tomlin Collection – 2nd Edition	$14.99
00702226	Chris Tomlin — See the Morning	$12.95
00148643	Train	$14.99
00702427	U2 — 18 Singles	$19.99
00702108	Best of Stevie Ray Vaughan	$17.99
00279005	The Who	$14.99
00702123	Best of Hank Williams	$15.99
00194548	Best of John Williams	$14.99
00702228	Neil Young — Greatest Hits	$17.99
00119133	Neil Young — Harvest	$14.99

Prices, contents and availability subject to change without notice.

HAL•LEONARD®

Visit Hal Leonard online at **halleonard.com**

1221
306